IN SEARCH OF WESTERN EUROPE

PEOPLE AND PLACES OF THE WORLD

IN SEARCH
OF
WESTERN EUROPE

Reader's
Digest

PUBLISHED BY THE READER'S DIGEST ASSOCIATION LIMITED
LONDON NEW YORK MONTREAL SYDNEY CAPE TOWN

Originally published in partwork form,
Des Pays et des Hommes,
by Librairie Larousse, Paris

A Reader's Digest selection

IN SEARCH OF WESTERN EUROPE

First English Edition Copyright © 1990
The Reader's Digest Association Limited, Berkeley Square House,
Berkeley Square, London W1X 6AB

Reprinted 1991

Copyright © 1990
Reader's Digest Association Far East Limited
Philippines Copyright 1990
Reader's Digest Association Far East Limited

Originally published in French as a partwork,
Des Pays et des Hommes
Copyright © 1984
Librairie Larousse

Translated and edited by Toucan Books Limited, London
Translator: Kitty Black

® Reader's Digest, The Digest and the Pegasus logo
are registered trademarks of
The Reader's Digest Association Inc. of Pleasantville, New York, USA

Typeset by Florencetype Ltd, Kewstoke, Avon
Printed in Spain

Contents

COVER PICTURES

Top: *The beautiful ruins of Castle Metternich are perched on the hillside overlooking the Mosel river in West Germany.*

Bottom: *A young boy and his grandfather bicycle home from the* boulangerie *in the French Pyrenees.*

The Heart of the Western World

Nowhere has seen more creative endeavour, or more self-destruction, than this leafy corner of the Eurasian land mass. No place on earth has fostered a greater ferment of cultures, or contributed more to the making of mankind. On a slant from alpine summit to irregular coastline sunk in mist and marsh, scoured by the ice ages, then picked over by wandering tribes, its landscape and pre-history hardly hint at the exceptional; geographers point to humid, temperate conditions that favoured cultivation, to an abundance of rivers, and to climate cycles that seemed to encourage in people a restless disposition: a restlessness that was to express itself in a need for change, for betterment, and in a persistent curiosity.

Civilisation came late here, though the grassy ramparts of forgotten strongholds and stone circles of forgotten religions, the many burial mounds and middens, remain to mark out activity before the Roman legions marched north to sort out the tribes at the point of the sword. But with the fall of Rome, the Roman cities and Roman roads became Roman ruins, and there was only the Church to sustain a little learning through dismal, disorganised dark ages. Charlemagne restored something of the old imperial unity when crowned Holy Roman Emperor in the year 800, but his empire soon crumbled into a rabble of feudal domains, with rapacious warfare the only enlivening element, and the marauding Crusades the nearest approximation to a united enterprise. The Crusades caused minds to look outwards, while contact with the 'infidel' Arab and Moor restored lost knowledge of a Roman heritage, and revealed the existence of new sciences, and discoveries in mathematics, astronomy, chemistry and medicine. That restless disposition could now be put to better use, particularly when the cultural spring of the Renaissance came bursting forth from Italy, to cause an extraordinary flowering of creativity in the 14th century.

The march from feudalism to freedom, from subsistence to a trading economy, was nevertheless gradual, with the Rhine, the Danube, and other great river-systems assuming the role of the old Roman roads. Ports and market towns proliferated as strongholds of a rich new merchant class, along with centres of specialisation so enduring that the name of a product is often better known than its place of origin – think of Gouda and Gruyère cheeses, Burgundy and Champagne wines, Charollais and Friesian cattle. The growth of the towns, and of larger political groupings, stimulated development in the arts and crafts, while regional farming techniques ensured that the landscape became richly differentiated.

With wealth to spend, and new nation-states to spend it, there was no stopping the restless spirit, and voyages of trade and discovery to the ends of the earth produced more riches and more ideas. The Pope determined upon a share-out of the new lands between Spain and Portugal, but the impossible, unruly, restless people across the Alps had unleashed the Reformation, and refused to be contained; it was said of the Dutch that they 'would trade with the devil in hell if they weren't afraid their sails would burn.' The plunder and the profit and the stimulation of conquest in turn made possible the spread of the industrial revolution; from France, through Belgium, into Germany, the vital coal deposits lay waiting to fuel the engines. The rest of Europe was left behind by all that was happening beyond the Alps, and by the 19th century, Western Europe (with its offshore islands) was exercising supremacy over the entire world. Everything about it became a model for other peoples' ambitions – its arts and monuments, its notions, expectations, prejudices, and politics were often the models to be copied. Progress was the watchword, and this vision of human perfectability still inspires much of the world, even though it was to prove a dangerous delusion. For out of the extraordinary success sprang the twin disasters of national rivalry and social dislocation, as old crafts were discarded and a disinherited underclass became the factory serfs of a new industrial feudalism. For the Congress of Vienna to succeed in 1815, a room had to be built with five great doorways, just so that the five great European powers could enter simultaneously. But no amount of adroit diplomacy could stop their rivalry from culminating in a world war, whose senseless slaughter only led to a further world war 21 years later. This time the sense of superiority born of success became so warped that it engendered a barbarity unmatched by any barbarism of the past.

If the shaming of German civilisation through the conduct of the Nazis brought Western Europe to its nadir, its resilience was never more evident than in the manner of its recovery from total ruination. With all pretensions to dominance gone (along with their colonies), and with outside superpowers now determining their fate, the shattered nations set about making sure that the past could not repeat itself. The dream was to achieve, in a friendly way, what only the Romans had achieved, and to replace the old nationalism with the supranationalism of a shared economy; with nothing to fight over, it was reasoned, there could be no more fighting.

It was appropriately in Rome, in 1957, that France, West Germany, the Netherlands, Belgium and Luxembourg joined with Italy in forming the European Community. Britain, sulking offshore, stayed away, and did not join until 17 years later; by then, it was clear that the Community was not only good for business, but was beginning to create a new kind of Europe. Super-motorways, fast trains, mass air-transport and abandoned customs-posts had dramatically reduced journey times, while fads and fashions swept through all the countries like a high wind, as did businessmen, entertainers and academics. Industries were merging across borders and it took an expert to tell one country's military uniform from another. Even national dishes were no longer sacrosanct; pizza parlours had begun to proliferate in the Champs Elysées, and supermarkets everywhere carried the same products. There was a downside, too, in traffic jams and dreary housing developments, but at least the telephones and the plumbing now worked.

Yet old ways die hard, and a shrinking Europe has only served to emphasise its extraordinary, and extraordinarily awkward, diversity. For some, the dream of unity remains a distant vision, and the Community little more than a fragile customs union, 'a mosaic of myopic, national, sacred egotisms badly harmonised,' as one Italian put it. Petty disputes fill the days of the bureaucrats – over, for instance, the size of lawnmowers; the French and Germans may have made up the quarrels of three wars, but agreeing on what constitutes mayonnaise is another matter. Profounder bigotries nestle deeply in minds, layer upon layer, nurtured, like the rich earth, through fifty generations of tilling. France, the most diverse and yet self-consciously nationalistic of countries, sees herself ruling the roost. In Belgium, Walloon and Fleming are meantime bound together in mutual hostility. At home in their mountain fastness, the Swiss tend to forget that they are Swiss at all, so fiercely do they identify with paternal village or valley, and it is as well to note that the official name of the country is not Switzerland, but Confederatia Helvetica, the confederation of the mountain tribes named the Helvetii by the Romans. Only tiny Luxembourg, a family as much as a nation, seems entirely at ease with the times, and only the Germans, sliced up by conquering armies, have striven as hard to become exemplary new Europeans.

Nevertheless, however you shake it, the European kaleidoscope contrives to dazzle as it constructs fresh patterns of inventive delight. 'Europe is no longer master of the world, but it is now an indispensable mistress, seductive, fecund, sparkling and consoling,' the American commentator Flora Lewis wrote in 1987. With the startlingly sudden meltdown of the Iron Curtain, and with tunnelers every day nearer to making Britain a physical part of the whole, the transformation is set to gather pace. In one of his more expansive moods, General de Gaulle once envisioned a united Europe extending 'from the Atlantic to the Urals.' This is no longer quite the wild fantasy that it was then.

France

France is a land of rich diversity. At one extreme, there are
the chilly mining towns of northern France; at the other, there
is the *maquis* of the South, where the landscape shimmers and glows
like a canvas by the painter Paul Cézanne. The differences between the two
halves of the country are greater than those of landscape alone.
In the Middle Ages they spoke different languages. And even today,
France appears to be a nation torn between Northern
Europe, on the one hand, and the Latin culture of
the Mediterranean on the other.

The **Pardon,** *the yearly visit to the parish shrine, is an occasion for Bretons to wear their traditional costume. There are hundreds of shrines and almost as many variations in costume. These, worn in Menez Hom, in Finistère, are almost monastic in their simplicity.*

Bicycling near Cheverny, in the beautiful Loire Valley, which the kings of France filled with fabulous castles.

Previous page: *Fireworks light up the sky above Notre Dame, the cathedral that has graced the heart of Paris for 800 years. This is Bastille Day, when the French celebrate the Fall of the Bastille prison on July 14, 1789, a key event in the French Revolution.*

From Brittany to Alsace

Modern France is a land of vineyards and lush, rolling farmlands. Its beautiful provincial cities and towns house fine restaurants and leisurely cafés. However, it is also a land of high-speed trains, a massive nuclear-reactor building programme, grandiose architectural projects and monumental traffic jams.

The largest country in western Europe has changed in many ways since the Second World War. A sudden spurt in the size of the French population after a half century of stagnation helped to prime the economic pump that has been sustained by the benefits of European economic integration. Now the citizens drink less wine but enjoy better quality. Over 10 per cent of families have a second home, and everyone is entitled to a minimum of five weeks' paid holiday a year. Even those rural areas that have retained their identity for centuries like Brittany in the north-west, Provence on the Mediterranean coast or Alsace on the German border have changed as French agriculture has modernised and the tiny peasant holdings of land have been amalgamated to form economic farming units; yet many of the old ways still survive. To understand this mixture of technological innovation and ancient local traditions, a little knowledge of French history is helpful.

Celtic tribes dominated western Europe as far south as modern Milan and Verona while Rome was just another rising city state. Only when Julius Caesar led his legions against these badly organised tribes between 58 and 50 BC did Roman ambitions succeed north of the Alps. However, as Rome's power started to fade in the 3rd century AD, attacks by Germanic tribes such as the Alemanni and the Franks disrupted the local administration and after the Huns sacked Rome in 455 the old order collapsed. Germanic tribes, each with its own language, moved in to fill the vacuum. The Visigoths took over territory along the Mediterranean and the Atlantic coast as far north as modern Bordeaux. The Burgundians controlled most of the Rhône Valley, while the Franks dominated the north.

From the end of the 5th century to the beginning of the 8th the Franks tried to conquer their neighbours but they were handicapped by their custom of dividing a dead king's territory equally among his sons. Only under their great military leader Charles Martel did they succeed in dominating a territory that included much of modern France, Germany and the Low Countries. Martel's grandson Charlemagne expanded on these triumphs and his conquests created an empire that extended from the Baltic in the north as far south as Corsica. However, the old rules of royal inheritance were revived and soon the Frankish Empire was dismembered, reviving the power of local leaders and traditions.

Meanwhile, the Vikings were expanding from their base in Scandinavia and in 911 the Frankish king Charles the Simple recognised their control of Normandy. Under William the Conqueror the Norman-Vikings overran England and in the process assumed a much more powerful position than their nominal king who only maintained firm control of the Ile-de-France region that surrounds modern Paris.

For much of the next 400 years the struggle for control of territory in central and northern France became a tug of war between these two groups, a struggle that was only resolved in 1453 when the English were finally ejected from all but the

The sheltered vineyards of the Jura produce a variety of wines. As well as red, white and rosé, there is a grey wine (actually a very pale rosé) and a splendid, aromatic vin jaune – *yellow wine.*

tiny fragment of France surrounding Calais. Nevertheless, that still left large areas of France beyond Parisian control. Picardy and Burgundy did not join the fold until 1477, while Anjou and Provence were not fully a part of France until 1481. Brittany did not acknowledge the French crown until 1532.

However, this still left as independent states important areas now part of modern France, particularly along the eastern border. The duchy of Lorraine was only finally annexed in 1766 while Savoy and the county of Nice did not become a permanent part of France until 1860. The last addition to mainland France took place in 1947, when Italy ceded the two Alpine communities of Brigue and Tende. It is, therefore, not surprising that many French regions have strong cultural traditions that are fiercely independent of Paris.

Today France is a republic that is divided into twenty-two regions that are the equivalent of English counties. These regions were set up during the 1960s. Each region is sub-divided into a number of departments, which follow the Napoleonic practice of taking their names from a nearby river or the local range of mountains; they have titles such as Seine-Maritime, Loiret, Lot-et-Garonne or Jura.

The people of many of these regions used to speak their own language but French became the language of everyday conversation as Paris came to control the country. Breton, which is closely related to Welsh and Gaelic, is still spoken in Brittany; in recent years a revived pride in Breton culture has encouraged the spread of Breton-speaking schools and state examinations set in the local language, as well as cultural festivals. But other languages such as Picard, Angevin and Burgundian are little more than names in history books.

The remains of the ancient forest of Gaul still survive in northern France. Magnificent oaks clothe the hills of the Ardennes close to the Belgian border in russet colours during the autumn, while pines and beeches cover the slopes of the department of the Vosges further south. In fact, over a quarter of France is still covered by woodland.

Many French forests have survived because the trees are growing on poor soils that would be uneconomic to clear and cultivate. However, much of the rest of the French countryside thrives upon very fertile soil that was cleared generations ago. Initially this ground was turned into the classic French open fields around which there were few hedges or fences. This unrestricted access arose from the system of early land use in France, in which fields were devoted to grazing animals one year and growing crops the next. When the field was being used for pasture, the local people could tether their animals upon it. When crops were being grown, the field was divided into narrow strips known as parcels with paths between them. Such a landscape can still be found in Lorraine and Alsace, near the border with Germany.

During the Middle Ages, as the idea of individual ownership began to supersede the communal possession of land, the state began to allow farmers to enclose their fields. As in Britain, stone walls were used in some parts of the country. However, in many places a more impenetrable barrier was created: either a hedge of interlaced shrubs and trees, a high earth bank or both. Such an enclosed field was known as a *bocage*. The typical *bocage* that relied purely on an impenetrable hedge could be found on the western fringes of the Paris region, while the most extreme form of a hedge set atop an earth bank can still be found in Brittany. It was this *bocage* landscape that proved such a barrier to the Allied advance through Normandy after the D-Day landings during the Second World War.

Durable, reliable slate roofs are a feature of the heavier rainfall areas of the north, but are much less evident in the south. Half the slates used in France come from quarries in the Anjou-Mayenne region.

Mayenne, noted for cattle and pigs, boasts farmsteads as elegant as manor houses, like this one with its charming pepperpot towers. Barns and granaries of shale and granite provide austere contrast.

Part of the landscape

Traditional French country houses take on the colours of their surroundings like chameleons. In Brittany they are made of granite and shale, like the rocks of the peninsula. The roofs are of slate: sombre and sober like the Atlantic clouds above. Bricks and tiles predominate in the north-east, left in their natural colours or whitewashed, with white or green shutters on the windows.

In Normandy, Champagne and Berry, the tradition of wooden-framed buildings with lath and plaster filling goes back to the days of the Roman Empire and was still commonly used in Normandy in the 19th century. The peasants grew the trees that went to make the frames which were generally built by carpenters who moved from site to site. In the Auge district in Normandy, the cobbing or daubing was made from a mixture of clay and straw, or clay and horsehair. In Alsace half-timbering was used extensively, and it was here that the craftsmen gave freest rein to their imagination by creating elaborate patterns with the wood.

In windy regions, the houses shelter against the sides of hills or are protected by screens of trees. They are low-set, like the sturdy little houses of the Breton coast, with steeply pitched roofs to shrug off the snow, a layer of pebble-dash to keep out the damp and thick walls to keep out the cold – granite in Brittany, sandstone in the Vosges mountains. In Picardy in the north-east the farms have flint and brick foundations as protection against the damp. In the Argonne, near the Belgian border, the roofs of the old houses project by as much as 6 feet, not only to keep the walls dry but to provide space where the harvest can be protected and stored. In parts of the Champagne region, small wooden scale-shaped tiles called tavillons are used on domestic as well as religious buildings to protect the walls – to very attractive effect.

Farm buildings were built and laid out according to local needs and customs. In Picardy, which grows mainly cereals and sugarbeet, the farm buildings are traditionally arranged round a square courtyard. The barns, which are pierced by gateways situated at either end, line the roadside. The stables, cow-sheds and pigsties are set at right angles to the barns, while the farmhouse completes the fourth side. This concentration of buildings saves on the construction of linking walls, gives good protection against the weather and minimises the effort expended on moving from job to job.

Yet this arrangement is not universal. In the Cauchois district, for instance, the buildings are scattered freely over the *masure*, a grassy area planted with fruit trees, surrounded by a ditch, with a screening of trees, which in Beubourg becomes a wall of clay and straw. In Normandy, men and animals never share the same buildings, even if they are set side by side, whereas in neighbouring Brittany the traditional layout means that they live under the same roof, separated sometimes only by a shale

The Alsace costume is a reminder of a province that was lost and regained from Germany twice in the past century, and which has been disputed territory for more than a thousand years. Alsatians have a dour, hard-working reputation and still speak their own dialect.

The traditional Alsatian house is encrusted with balconies and steep roofs with pointed gables. Its inviting warmth belies the grim history of the region, where some of the major battles of the First World War were fought.

partition or a wall fitted up as a manger.

Even simpler are the Breton fishermen's homes, which huddle close together for protection against the Atlantic storms. A little further south the houses of the water meadows of north Vendée are made of a mixture of clay and reeds or straw without any wooden framework; the walls are built up directly on a raised bank without proper foundations.

Warm and comfortable

From the Vendée on the west coast to the Ardennes in the east, before the invention of modern heating systems, family life in northern France revolved round the fire in the living room. In Brittany, poor families only had one room where three generations would eat and sleep. The privacy of each group was protected by their box beds which were completely enclosed in shuttered wooden partitions. However, such limited resources were the exception, and most traditional French houses had more than one room.

Close to the Swiss border in the Franche-Comté region, farms and town houses had two main rooms, the *housteau*, which was used as kitchen, communal room or living room, and the *poêle*, a room heated by

The tall, wide, deep and elaborately carved Normandy cupboard was originally intended to hold a bride's trousseau, and always featured in the marriage contract. It came to symbolise a family's wealth.

The name Normandy evokes images of soft pastures and little apple orchards. This crop may be turned into cider, the favourite local drink, which is distilled to make the celebrated apple brandy called calvados, often the secret ingredient that adds fire and flavour to the formidable Normandy dinner.

Garlic is an important ingredient in many traditional French dishes. This farmer is loading the boxes which will be sent off to many local markets.

a stove where the parents or grandparents slept but where the family also entertained. The beds were either half-hidden or curtained off, and the children and servants slept in the attics or in the barns.

The stove is still used in Lorraine but in that region the arrangement of the rooms – and there were and usually still are at least three – was different. Each one opened off a corridor, or sometimes a barn, while the kitchen, often windowless, was placed behind a glass partition. In neighbouring Alsace the room known as the *stube*, heated by a special stove, now mostly has a radiator, like the rest of the rooms. Replacing the open fireplaces of the 15th century, the stove became a decorative feature and today is much sought after by collectors and museums.

The furniture standing in these rooms also reflects the customs and culture of each region. Owing to the distances involved, Parisian styles filtered through only gradually, so provincial cabinetmakers remained faithful to the 17th-century styles of Louis XIII and the opulence of the 18th century under Louis XVI well into the 20th century. Chests, heavy cupboards, dressers and huge tables were made from local wood, sometimes ostentatiously carved with the owner's name, initials and wedding date.

In Brittany, the bride was expected to bring her own box bed as part of her dowry to give her a certain independence, so that her husband could never tell her 'You're sleeping in my bed!' Traditionally, and it is still very much the case even today, the moving of the young couple's furniture into their new home provides the occasion for much rejoicing and – with the help of a liberal supply of wine – a great deal of noise. In Normandy and Alsace the move by the young couple was also a very public occasion, as the families wanted to demonstrate their status to the new neighbours.

A special significance was attached to some pieces of furniture and their use. For instance, the most comfortable chair was reserved for the 'master of the house', who was the first to take his place at table, thereby giving the rest of the household permission to be seated. Furniture is also associated with superstition. It is not considered lucky to lean on the table and this may be the reason why French parents tirelessly exhort their offspring not to put their elbows on the table. Creaking produced by changes in the weather is taken to signify warnings of disaster. In Alsace, all the furniture is changed round after a death. One widespread custom, which was recorded quite recently, consists of stopping the clock at the exact moment when a member of the household dies and only starting it up again when the family returns from the cemetery.

Picking cauliflowers in Morlaix. Lapped on three sides by the Gulf Stream, Brittany enjoys a mild winter and is renowned for its early vegetables. It produces three-quarters of the French cauliflower crop. Long considered a poor relation of the more prosperous French provinces, Brittany is now catching up.

Nowadays, as prosperity has grown and people change jobs and homes more frequently than in the past, fewer than 50 per cent of French people still live in the department in which they were born. This would tend to undermine local traditions, but behaviour has changed less than might be expected. If brides no longer bring their beds with them as part of their dowry, in many parts of the country they embroider their trousseaux during the summer holidays while they are still at school or university. And in the north, for instance, the presents given to girls on their 15th birthdays by parents and grandparents, godmothers and godfathers, are often intended for use during their married life.

From peasant to businessman

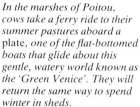

In the marshes of Poitou, cows take a ferry ride to their summer pastures aboard a plate, *one of the flat-bottomed boats that glide about this gentle, watery world known as the 'Green Venice'. They will return the same way to spend winter in sheds.*

The rich traditions of French rural life often concealed considerable hardship as families fought to gain a living from tiny plots using the most primitive equipment and techniques. However, over the last 100 years the number of farms has dwindled – from 5.7 million in 1892 to just over 1 million today. As the amount of agricultural land is still approxim-

ately the same at 124,000 square miles, which is over twice the amount of land used for farming in western Germany, individual French farms have obviously grown in size.

Changing techniques have also made a considerable difference to the French rural scene, particularly since the Second World War. French farmers owned only 44,000 tractors in 1946 but the American government's Marshall Plan, which was designed to aid European reconstruction in the post-war years, first helped the French to import large numbers of American tractors and then encouraged them to build factories so that they could manufacture their own. Nowadays France has over 1.5 million tractors.

The post-war revolution in biotechnology also helped the French to increase the yield from their land. For example, not only did the introduction of new sweetcorn hybrids double the yield on existing fields, it also allowed the crop to be grown in northern France because the new strains needed fewer hours of sunshine to ripen. Improvements in veterinary knowledge led to a doubling of milk yields and an increase in the number of animals that could be grazed on an acre of land.

The improvements have had their greatest effect in the north and north-west of France where the

country's most fertile land is located. Brittany, which used to be practically isolated, has become the leading producer of turkeys, pigs and poultry, while France is now Europe's second largest centre of dairy farming, much of which is concentrated in Normandy. This growth has led to the development of a vigorous agrochemical industry which provides local jobs for a certain number of the younger generation and those who have ceased to cultivate the land themselves.

Fertilisers, expensive machinery and farming methods worked out on computers are required by huge organisations working thousands of hectares, as in the Aisne district of the Picardy region. This is far removed from the classic image of the peasant providing food for his family by the sweat of his brow. Yet, in this changing world traces of the past still appear at every turn. In the department of Loiret south of Paris, or Brittany in the west, harvest festi-

Producing grapes for the earthy, opulent wines of Burgundy demands constant hard work: hoeing, harrowing, weeding, fertilising, tying, pruning and constant spraying. Here the pruned cuttings are being burned at Nuits-St-Georges, a famous name sustained on little more than 900 acres of land. To the north and south are other great names of Burgundy: Chambertin, Clos de Vougeot, Vosne-Romanée and Chambolle Musigny.

France has few navigable rivers, but an immense network of canals, constructed mainly in the 17th century. Many were left to deteriorate as rail and road captured the commercial traffic, but now they have become popular with holidaymakers. They are so much a part of the landscape that it is difficult to imagine a time without them.

On the extreme western tip of France, on a promontory 1500 feet above the Atlantic breakers, Our Lady of the Shipwrecks stands as a divine sentinel for the fishermen who wrest a precarious living from the sea. Life is hard on the little trawlers, with only a few hours' rest between trips. Though France has 3400 miles of coastline and the French eat a considerable amount of fish, demand is falling and fishing is a declining industry.

vals, with everyone wearing traditional costumes, are always crowded – sometimes staged for the benefit of the tourists, but more often purely for local enjoyment. Windmills have been restored and their sails are turning again. In the Vendée, the mill at Châteauneuf still grinds between 50 and 60 kg of flour every hour. In Loiret a society has been formed dedicated to the restoration of these survivals of the past, like the mills at Pelard, Bois de Feugères, Bouville, Levesville-la-Chenard, Moutiers and Ouarville. The same is happening in the north, in the Pas-de-Calais and the Somme.

The men of the sea

France has a long coastline and if the sea spray does not reach as far as Paris, the changing skies and showers brought by the west wind do sweep in to dowse it unhindered. From the Belgian frontier to the mouth of the Loire at St Nazaire on the Atlantic, ports great and small succeed each other – fishing ports, industrial complexes, merchant and naval bases: Dunkirk, Calais, Boulogne, Le Havre,

St Malo, Brest and many more. The lives of a good proportion of the population are governed by the tides or the rhythmic arrivals and departures of the many boats.

Men from the island of Sein off the tip of Brittany are at sea from June to September tunny fishing in the Gulf of Gascony or the Irish Sea, or working on the freezer ships on their long voyages down the coast of Africa. The men of St Malo, heirs of the corsairs and *terre-neuvas*, the boats that sailed to Newfoundland to fish off the Grand Banks, still go after cod for three months in far-off northern waters in boats fitted with refrigeration units. The men of Lorient in Brittany sign on with the factory boats, ranging from 50 to 700 tons, which fish for hake in the seas north of Ireland and Scotland and as far away as the Faroes.

For all these fishermen the modernisation of their equipment has not meant the end of their labours – quite the contrary. Working for 16 hours out of 24, they spend weeks away from their families. After months at sea, a modern *terre-neuva* only stays in port for three weeks before setting out again. However, to increase the revenue from long-haul fishing and to improve living conditions for the men, an attempt has been made by the companies based in Lorient to extend the time the ships remain at sea by using air travel to rotate the crews while resupplying the boats by sea.

Individual ownership is less demanding on the crew since a trawler that lacks a back-up organisation will probably spend no more than two or three days at sea. Paradoxically such small units have been affected less by economic difficulties than industrialised fishing has. If demand for the bulk species such as cod and hake falls off, the smaller boats can concentrate on lobsters and shellfish or those fish such as sole, skate and sea bream which can only be caught in relatively small numbers but which command a high price.

Mussels have been cultivated in the muddy bay of Aiguillon, near La Rochelle, for more than eight hundred years. This method, said to have been introduced by a shipwreckèd Irish sailor in 1235, involves driving piles (bouchots) into the seabed. The mussels attach themselves to the piles and are collected at low tide.

Men of iron

The Gauls were always expert metalworkers. The name Ferrière, meaning a deposit of iron or a forge, appears everywhere in the north, especially in Normandy. Near Ouche in Burgundy the iron-masters used to live in hamlets on the outskirts of the Forest of Breteuil; each had his own speciality – household, marine or saddlery accessories. In Brittany, the forges were located in the forests of Paimpont or in the south of the region at Hennebont, which only closed as late as 1968. The forges at La Chaussade, in the Creuse, and Guérigny in the Nièvre, were among the largest in France in the 18th century and they only closed down at the beginning of the 1970s.

But French steel was – and still is – mainly centred in Lorraine, whose prosperity rested on the industry for nearly a century. The workers formed the spearhead of the trades union movement and their wages were always used as a benchmark for the rest of the working population. During the 1960s new production records were set, reaching a peak in 1962 with an output of 62 million tons. Then came the world steel crisis, which was caused by over-investment in new plant, and the market collapsed. By 1979 production in Lorraine had fallen to less than half its previous level, causing mines and factories to close. Retraining and redeployment of the workers is difficult because of the intense specialisation of the area: in some communities more than half the working population was employed in steel.

The industry had a marked effect on the landscape as well as on the minds of its people. Few green fields were to be seen in the area, just tall chimneys and 'dark Satanic mills'. And the many immigrant workers, mostly between 20 and 49 years of age, will find it difficult to move into new areas for much of the rest of French heavy industry is experiencing its own difficulties. Coal mining, the other traditional industry in the east, is also going through some tough times.

French mines are not easy to work and not very profitable. The legendary black faces are disappearing. In 1946 there were 300,000 miners but by 1983 the number was down to 57,000 and is still dropping. Early retirement is one solution, 40 now being the accepted age as opposed to the previous age limit of 50. But that leads to great dissatisfaction among those who are dismissed. Of course it was a hard life with long hours spent underground, bringing the risk of accidents and lung disease. But it also had advantages that balanced the equation: generous social security, a feeling of solidarity and the kind of fellowship among the miners that was unknown in other jobs.

Steel and coal are two examples of the difficult situation faced by French industry which, as in other developed countries, is going through a period of readjustment. Textiles, chemicals, the car and aerospace industries are faced with many problems. Fortunately the men of the north lack neither courage nor energy, as shown by their towns and cities which have been invaded so many times over the centuries. Yet, despite their misfortunes, the people have maintained their traditions and way of life. Lille, Metz, Nancy, Strasbourg, to name only the largest, are welcoming cities which are proud of their past and, in spite of the troubled times, confident in the future.

However, in France there is always one solution to local unemployment. If there is no work in the provinces, jobs can always be found around Paris where, in spite of all the French government's efforts at decentralisation, the major part of French economic life is centred. In France, all roads lead not to Rome but to the capital.

Belfries, the watchtowers of past ages, have become the symbol of municipal independence in northern France. Were the burghers ever again to require men at arms, the Union of Archers of the North of France has a plentiful supply, with more than 68 member associations!

There is a wariness in the eyes of this miner from Lens. He and the other 'black faces' have an uncertain future. Life in the north has revolved around coal, but now the industry is declining.

A typical northern landscape. In the shadow of the mine-dumps, flowers soften some of the industrial scars and the neat houses have freshly painted woodwork. Many French workers now own their own homes.

A terrace café on the Champs-Elysées is the essence of Paris life to many people. Cafés are open all day and are generally the last places to close at night, and so they are the ideal place for meetings, or reflective contemplation. Yet there can be great loneliness in the midst of such bustle.

Paris is still dominated by the gigantic rebuilding programme undertaken by Baron Haussmann in the 19th century. Its citizens took time to grow accustomed to the distinctive silhouette of the Eiffel Tower, but what was once an outlandish novelty has become one of the best-loved symbols of Paris.

Living in Paris

Paris is the heart and soul, the showcase and trademark of France. In the days when France dominated Europe, the city was looked on as the capital of the civilised world. Those times are past but Paris still retains its magic. A Canadian, a Brazilian or a Japanese tourist visiting Europe would think twice before missing the Eiffel Tower, Montmartre, Notre-Dame, the Louvre and the Invalides, the Pompidou Centre and Pigalle.

However, if foreigners visit the main monuments, take a trip in a riverboat, a *bateau-mouche*, past some of the scenes of the most important moments in the history of France, go window-shopping in the rue du Faubourg St Honoré, perhaps enjoy a snack in a café on the Champs-Elysées, or stroll in the Luxembourg Gardens, they will not learn very much about the real Paris. Its citizens have little time to spare for strangers and their private lives, like their homes, are only rarely opened to them.

The bridges of Paris have a romantic aura of their own. The Pont des Arts was the first in the city to be made of iron and was finished in 1804, though the original had to be replaced after it was damaged by a barge.

French porcelain has been made at Sèvres, south-west of Paris, ever since Madame de Pompadour persuaded Louis XV to have the factory moved there in the mid-18th century. Since the time of Napoleon, the wares have been gilded. Presentation pieces are made for foreign heads of state.

Tourists also tend to keep to the better-known areas of Paris. They rarely visit the districts which, like so many small villages, cluster inside the great city – Auteuil, the Batignolles, the Buttes-Chaumont, the Marais, the Gobelins, Saint-Germain-des-Prés. Instead they will carry away an impression of dense traffic and the headlong flight of pedestrians who are frequently rather rude. They rarely discover the quiet, almost provincial streets, where everyone takes their dog for a walk in the evening. The number of dogs in the street creates great cleansing problems for the local authorities but earns fortunes for dog food manufacturers and the owners of veterinary clinics and animal beauty parlours.

Parisians will tell you that their way of life is mad and always wonder why they do not sell up and go and live in the country. In fact, over the last few decades the city has lost some of its population. But people have merely moved out into the surrounding districts of the Ile-de-France, which today has a population of over 10 million.

However, many people live in the suburbs not from choice but from necessity. Housing is very scarce in central Paris and rents are higher than elsewhere - apart from the smart suburbs to the west of the city, like Neuilly, the nearest and most sought after. The new high-speed underground, the RER (Réseau Express Régional) has made a considerable improvement to the links between Paris and the suburbs, making it possible to live further and further afield. New towns, such as Evry, Cergy-Pontoise and Marne-la-Vallée, have sprung up in the middle of green fields, and efforts are being made to build high-rise blocks that are less stark than the box-like towers erected in the 1950s and 1960s. The classic small suburban villa of the years between the wars has often been replaced by houses that are charming enough, but endlessly repetitious.

If suburbanites have to get up early to go to work in the capital, Parisians cannot always start much later. Even if they live in the centre of the city they may have to make long journeys to reach their office, workplace or shop. Morning and evening, employers, employees, executives and students cram into the buses and swamp the Métro.

Paris also has a rapidly increasing immigrant population – former colonial subjects from Senegal or Mali, Algerians and Cambodians, Vietnamese and even Pakistanis, who have taken advantage of the freedom of movement within the European Community to cross the Channel. Newcomers from Africa generally live in the poorer quarters like the 19th and 20th postal districts on the eastern rim of the city and the 18th on the north side, which is

nicknamed 'The Drop of Gold' but is considerably less poetic than it sounds. Oriental immigrants usually live in the south-east of the city in the 13th district near the avenue d'Italie. However, the largest immigrant group in France comes from Portugal and many of them work as janitors, looking after offices and blocks of flats.

Generally speaking, the wealthy live in the districts close to Notre-Dame, the 4th, near to the Eiffel Tower, the 7th, or close to the Bois de Boulogne, the 16th. The intellectuals live south of the River Seine on what is always known as the Left Bank in the 5th and 6th districts close to the University of the Sorbonne. Montparnasse, which used to be where all the artists lived, is now home to enormous office blocks, cinemas and theatres. North of the Seine, next to the Place de la Bastille, is the Marais which has a small Jewish quarter – little delicatessens sell kosher meat while restaurants serve central and eastern European specialities. The business section is centred round the Bourse (the Stock Exchange), the Opéra and the Gare St Lazare, in the 8th district to the north of the Louvre, and at La Défense with its immense steel and glass constructions worthy of Manhattan, just outside the western limits of the city.

The glass towers of La Défense reflect the spirit of a new Paris. Built where a monument once stood to commemorate the defence of the capital in 1871, this development to the west of the city has 10 million square feet of office space, 12,000 living units, a vast commercial centre and landscaped parks.

Behind the Pompidou Centre, in the area where the ancient market of Les Halles once stood, blocks of flats have been built to reflect the style of the old houses of the district, most of which have been renovated. The Centre itself, with its naked piping, is in startling contrast to everything around it. It is the most-visited building in Europe, both for its novelty and for the magnificent modern art collection that it houses.

Small bistros and great restaurants

Parisians who have not had time to eat breakfast before leaving home may stop on the way to work for the traditional white coffee and croissant. Many will come back to the same bistro for their midday meal, if they have no canteen or if they have not been converted to the merits of fast food. The set-price meal will usually consist of steak and chips, unless the 'day's special' is Alsatian sauerkraut and sausage, *boeuf bourguignon* (beef stewed in red wine) or *blanquette de veau* (veal in a white wine, cream and

onion sauce), all washed down by a carafe of house wine or a glass of beer.

This meal bears no relation to the business lunch given by the managing director or the business manager for colleagues or clients. In the luxurious atmosphere of a famous Parisian restaurant, the maître d'hôtel will produce a menu which can prove bewildering to the foreign visitor. Even if he thinks he understands French, he will not necessarily know what to expect from a *cassolette de ris de veau aux petites morilles* (casserole of sweetbreads with wild mushrooms) or a *gratin de cailles de vigne aux truffes* (quails with truffles and breadcrumbs). Choosing a wine is even more difficult, especially if the visitor is from a country where it is rarely drunk. As for the cheese – France produces no fewer than 350 varie-

ties, though fortunately the cheeseboard will only include a few samples.

A business lunch can easily go on until 3.30 or 4 o'clock in the afternoon, by which time most employees will start to think about going home, especially if there is some shopping to do. Or perhaps there's time to look in at the latest exhibition at the Grand Palais. Close by, the cinemas of the Champs-Elysées advertise all the latest films on the basis of an

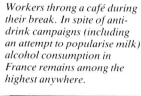

Workers throng a café during their break. In spite of anti-drink campaigns (including an attempt to popularise milk) alcohol consumption in France remains among the highest anywhere.

A demonstration at the Citröen factory. The French car industry employs many foreigners, who are anxious about their job security. The introduction of robots is something that makes them particularly uneasy.

exclusive presentation and on Friday and Saturday nights long queues form on the pavement outside.

Parisians do not go to the theatre as often as they used to, although the tradition of buying season tickets for the Comédie-Française, the French equivalent of the National Theatre, is maintained in certain families. Enthusiasts seem to prefer those performances given in uncomfortable and draughty surroundings in the suburbs by the 'fringe' groups.

Other very different entertainments still flourish – the Folies-Bergères, the Moulin Rouge and the Crazy Horse Saloon – but are more popular with provincials and foreigners than with the native Parisians who have often never set foot inside any of them.

Sunset in the rue Mouffetard. In the shadow of the church of St Médard, a typical Paris street market flourishes.

Beautiful August

At the weekend, Parisians can put in a little jogging in the Bois de Boulogne or the Bois de Vincennes. They can take their children to the zoo, or the Jardin d'Acclimatisation where there is a farm with ducks, chickens and pigs. They can go for a stroll down the wide avenues laid out by Baron Haussmann in the last century or look at the new boutiques in the Forum des Halles on the site of the old meat and vegetable markets. But more often than not, except in the depths of winter, the family will leave town for the weekend if they are lucky enough to have a little place somewhere in the Ile-de-France or otherwise just spend Sunday in the country.

The problem is not driving out of town, it is getting back, with cars bumper to bumper for mile after mile. By the time they get back to town they will be more on edge than when they set out.

Fortunately most people can look forward to their annual holiday to escape from the crush. From July 14, Paris empties. This is the time when lovers of the city have it to themselves – no cars, no crowded pavements, no trucks or lorries. The golden August sun gives it a special brilliance and the trees in the avenues are barely tinged with the first signs of autumnal colour.

While tourists cool down beside the fountains of the Trocadéro, a few yards away they may be startled to see a young woman muffled in a thick woollen coat, wearing fur boots, striking poses in front of the Eiffel Tower following the commands of a photo-grapher. She is a model, of course, for the winter collections are being prepared in the salons of the great couturiers. In spite of competition from Rome, Milan, London and New York, Paris is still a major force in the fashion world.

In a more macabre vein, Paris is also a city of elaborate tombstones and ornate cemeteries of which the most famous is Père Lachaise. There you will find the tombs of Molière and La Fontaine, Balzac, Chopin, Beaumarchais and Sarah Bernhardt, to name just a few. Local people use it like a park and stroll along the green paths among the monuments. While senior citizens gossip on the benches, lovers pause in front of the mausoleum raised to the memory of the most famous couple in medieval history, Héloïse and Abélard.

Paris is all this and much more – the young guitar player in the Métro, a jeweller's shop in the Place Vendôme, an historic building in the Marais. It is bookstalls on the banks of the Seine and café tables on the pavement where the talk sparkles and bubbles. However, perhaps Paris bubbles less than it did as it has come to resemble other great cities. Who would have thought 20 years ago that French people would buy hamburgers on the Champs-Elysées?

Perhaps it needs a special occasion to make the city fizz again – the bicentenary of the Republic, a visit from the British royal family, especially the Princess of Wales, the finish of the Tour de France cycle race. Then, for a few hours, the city hums and vibrates and all the grandeur of the past is revived in the present.

The Forum des Halles. For centuries Les Halles was the 'stomach' of Paris, the site of the meat, fruit and vegetable markets, but in 1969 they were all moved out to Rungis, and that was the end of the revellers who rounded off the night by eating onion soup in one of the workers' bars. Wrought-iron market stands were torn down and replaced by these boutiques.

The Luminous South

The lands stretching from the Pyrenees to the Alps, from the Gironde estuary on the Atlantic coast to the Mediterranean are as varied as their names. The French language seems to be the only common denominator that covers the whole of the South, also known as the Midi. However, the dialects spoken in Provence, Auvergne or Gascony are very different from one another, although they all started from a common root. So where is the South dreamed of by the people living in colder, more dismal haunts, the land of sunshine and blue skies? In fact there is not one but many 'souths', their aspects changing according to their situation and climate.

Close to the Mediterranean coastline, dry and luminous, the Midi shimmers and glows like a canvas by Paul Cézanne, the greatest painter of the South. Here rocks seem to triumph over vegetation. To the pitiless pressure of nature has been added the careless actions of men who cleared the land by deliberately starting fires to destroy the primeval forest and allowed their sheep and goats to graze everywhere. Now, thyme, lavender and rosemary flourish on the limestone hills among the stunted oaks. Elsewhere the flinty soil is covered by the vegetation known as the *maquis*, with its cork and evergreen oaks, dwarf pines, tree heather and broom. The air is filled with sweet scents and the song of the cicadas. At higher altitudes, between 2600 and 6000 feet, the *maquis* gives way to deciduous oaks, sweet chestnuts, beech and ash.

Along the Mediterranean coast, between Provence in the east and the Languedoc in the west, the twin arms of the Rhône delta embrace the Camargue, a primitive world where sky, land and water seem to merge and pink flamingoes flap up from the shallows when disturbed by herds of wild bulls driven by riders mounted on white horses. Even more authentically Mediterranean is Corsica, only reluctantly a French possession: a mountainous island with a wild beauty, the sea pounding relentlessly against its rocky coast.

The western rim of the Midi facing the Atlantic presents a very different picture. This is the ancient

Lavender must be picked carefully, for the bushes may shelter snakes. Cultivation of the fragrant plants in the Alps of Haute Provence was started after the First World War. Now the job can be done mechanically.

In the Bethmale Valley, men and women used to wear these wooden sabots. At Christmas, a young man of the Valley would give his betrothed a pair that he had carved himself; the longer the points, the deeper his love was supposed to be.

The annual migration of cattle and sheep is a feature of Mediterranean life that still goes on in the south of France. In June, when the winter pastures begin to be scorched by the sun, the animals are driven to the higher meadows. Nowadays they usually make the trip by rail or lorry, but this flock on the road to Col d'Allos is doing it the old way.

The shepherd's life might seem to be idyllic, free and in harmony with nature, but that is not the whole story: there is also the discomfort, the loneliness, and the monotony of the job to consider.

The night before leaving for the mountains, wooden collars with bells attached are fastened round the necks of the most prized animals. Some sheep also have coloured woollen pompoms tied to their backs.

kingdom of Aquitaine, a triangle hemmed in by the high plateaux of the Massif Central, the Pyrenees and the ocean. Here the sunshine is less prodigal than on the Côte d'Azur with an annual average of 2000 hours, as opposed to 3000 enjoyed by the Mediterranean coast.

There is enormous variety in the landscapes of this region, ranging from the sandy wastes of the Landes – today covered by the largest forest in France – to the windswept, stony expanses of the limestone plateaux of the Causses, about 70 miles north-west of Nîmes. Between these two extremes lie hidden green valleys or wide plains golden in summer with ripening wheat. Around Bordeaux the grape reigns supreme, with row after row of perfectly aligned vines clothing the rolling slopes. In spite of a turbulent history that includes religious suppression, the Black Death, centuries of allegiance to the English crown and the religious wars of the 15th and 16th centuries, Aquitaine has prospered.

With the Pyrenees forming a barrier to the south, the Alps closing the frontier to the east and the solid bloc of the Massif Central in between, southern France can appear to be a world of mountains: high

peaks, closed valleys or fertile plains rimmed with crags. As they approach the Mediterranean the mountains take on its luminous and changing colours. The Pyrenees plunge into the sea at Banyuls, followed by the St Baume range further down the coast. Then comes the Massif des Maures reaching the sea to the east of Toulon; the red rocks of the Esterel between St Tropez and Nice; and, eventually, the Maritime Alps. At higher altitudes the mountains become starker and colder, clothed with forests of silver fir and pine and sparse Alpine grasses, until everything gives way to the barren world of the highest peaks.

Savoy was one of the last independent kingdoms to be united with France – in 1860. But long before then its language, traditions and legal system made it very French. Pressed against the Swiss and Italian Alps, it is often cut off by snow during the winter, yet this region has been the crossroads between Italy and France since Roman times.

Further south, the Dauphiné has been an integral part of France since the 14th century, even though it only came under direct French control a century later. Stendhal, one of the greatest of French writers, evoked its mountains and the River Isère in the early 19th century when he wrote that it 'watered the rich greenery of the most fertile and best cultivated plain

in the land'. Nowadays the Isère Valley would not be considered particularly rich and Stendhal would certainly not recognise his birthplace, Grenoble. In his time it produced gloves and straw hats; nowadays it prefers electronics, telecommunications and nuclear research and is one of the fastest-growing cities in France.

Daughters of Rome

In these southern lands linked with ancient civilisations many of the towns remain deeply marked by the Roman influence, particularly in Provence and the Languedoc, where on the narrow coastal strip the settlements clustered, grew and prospered. Vaison, Arles, Nîmes, St Rémy and Orange are the jewels in the ancient crown of Provence, for they have carefully preserved all traces of the Roman occupation. The same is not true of Aix, though it is still one of the most beautiful cities in France with its squares centred on sparkling fountains, its aristocratic old houses of the 17th and 18th centuries and the warm tones of its stone walls.

Marseilles dates from an even earlier period for it was founded by Greek colonists around 600 BC, but

The 'old port' of Marseilles is used mainly by pleasure craft, now that the fishing port has been moved to the north end of the bay. But fishermen are still on hand to sell the gurnard, scorpion-fish, sea bream, catfish and mullet that go into the making of bouillabaisse, *the chunky fish-soup of the region.*

it carries its 26 centuries lightly. The second city of France is still the leading port in the Mediterranean, in spite of French decolonisation and the decline of the national merchant shipping fleet.

Dreaming of more recent times, Nice remembers the days when in winter it played host to Russian princes and English aristocrats who built the extravagant villas of the Belle Epoque before the First World War. But like all the other towns on the Côte d'Azur, it has had to cope with fresh waves of tourists with less money and less elegant tastes in recent times. As a result it has lost some of its charm, like so many of its neighbours. St Tropez was once a peaceful fishing village, not the summertime circus of titillation it has become today.

Further west, Toulouse, now the great centre of the French aerospace industry, has grown considerably in the last 30 years. The fine houses in pink brick built in the old days by rich burghers and municipal magistrates are surrounded by modern constructions which do not conform to the same aesthetic considerations. However, this does not stop the Toulousains – the old-established as well as the newcomers – from loving their bustling, animated and sun-drenched city.

Bordeaux, the other great industrial city of the south-west, is more reserved. It became an English possession when Eleanor of Aquitaine married Henry Plantagenet and remained under the English crown for three hundred years, during which time its wine growers made fortunes by exporting their vintages to England. Later, in the 18th century, it became even richer thanks to the sugar industry and the slave trade.

Clermont-Ferrand, capital of the Auvergne, owes its fortune to the Michelin brothers who, at the end of the 19th century, founded France's rubber manufacturing industry there. In the city centre, in the Place de Jaude, is an equestrian statue of Vercingetorix, the hero of the struggle against the Romans. That his conquerors enjoyed the mineral springs in the region has been demonstrated by the remains excavated in spas such as Vichy, Le Mont-Dore, Royat, Chaudes-Aigues and even Lyons.

In Marseilles, as elsewhere in the south, a game of cards means gambling, and that means argument. The 19th-century writer Jules Michelet said of Provence: 'It is the land of fine talkers, voluble and passionate.'

Pétanque, *the national game of Provence, is played in the shade of the plane trees at sunset, or after the siesta. They say you need to be born in Provence and be fond of* pastis *to become a good* pétanque *player.*

In Lozère the community continues to dwindle. The peasant population of France dropped from 21 per cent in 1962 to 3 per cent in 1991.

Lyons, the first capital of Gaul, was built at the junction of two great rivers, the foaming Rhône and the peaceful Saône, and at the meeting place of two worlds, the south and the north. Nowadays Lyons is a great industrial centre, although it is also famous for the Beaujolais wine that it exports – the third river that runs through the town according to some. It is proud of its Place Bellecoeur, its old St-Jean district and the new district of the Part-Dieu, though probably less proud of the Catholic basilica, perched on the hill of Fourvière, a scene which has been described as an elephant lying on its back. Directly opposite the hill of Fourvière is the hill of the Croix-Rousse, which in the 19th century was known as the 'Acropolis of silk'. Here, in miserable conditions, the weavers lived and made the fabulous silks and damasks for which Lyons was famous. They demonstrated in the 1830s for a rise in pay and fought furiously in the *traboules*, the labyrinth of narrow streets and stairways so characteristic of the Croix-Rousse district.

Building a home

As in northern France, southern building materials vary greatly according to the locality: the grey slate and stone of Limousin, the rugged granite of the Auvergne, the brilliant white limestone of the Loire Valley and the pink roofs of Provence, Languedoc or Gascony. The visitor can enjoy the glowing beauty of Toulousain stone under the rays of the setting sun, the ancient façades of the Dordogne or the dazzle of pebble-dashed, whitewashed Basque houses in the shadow of the Pyrenees.

There are also vast architectural differences be-

The remains of an old fort can be seen above La Garde-Freinet, a village guarding a pass in the thickly wooded Massif des Maures, once held by Saracen invaders.

tween the various regions. In the Dordogne the simplest farm may have a roof with dormer windows worthy of a manor house, just for the fun of it. The houses in Corsica are often very tall and narrow, in complete contrast to the classic low Provençal farmhouse, known as a *mas*. This will have a main room, a kitchen and bread oven on the ground floor, with outbuildings for the animals and farm equipment and a single storey above for the bedrooms and store rooms. The stone-built houses of the Cévennes, the mountain range sandwiched between the Massif Central and the Provençal coastline, are often carved out of the living rock. They rarely have their entrance at the front, which is fitted with narrow windows. Instead it is situated at the side – a souvenir of the days when strangers were viewed with suspicion. However, in Toulouse the houses have wide, double front doors which seem to offer a welcome to visitors. As for the houses around

Bordeaux, they prefer to hide their wealth behind their vines.

In Savoy and Dauphiné, as in all mountainous regions, the house represents a struggle against nature. Heavy snowfalls, cold, ice, rain and floodwaters all have to be taken into consideration. Every high-altitude village is a challenge to nature.

The growth of winter sports which has transformed peaceful villages into fashionable ski resorts, has been a mixed blessing. The shepherd has become the ski instructor, while speculators put up square cabins copied from industrial centres or rows of 'minichalets'. The removal of conifers to make ski runs has destabilised the snow and increased the danger of avalanches.

In many villages the old patterns still survive as houses cluster round the church as if to borrow warmth and comfort, stretch out along the main street or scatter over the south-facing slopes. With

A scene in Corrèze, 50 miles west of Clermont-Ferrand. Mobile shops are a new feature of country life, and replace the shopkeepers and tradesmen who have departed with the depopulation of many small villages. They provide a focal point for daily gossip.

only limited space available in the village, the houses are usually built on several levels: cowsheds on the ground floor, living rooms on the first floor and storehouses under the tiles. However, the new way of life means that very often the first level has been left free, with the animals installed in outbuildings.

In the Haute Auvergne the same arrangement has been followed with the top floor being used as a hay-loft, which helps to insulate the household from the winter cold. As a final refinement, a trapdoor is located so that it only needs to be opened to allow the fodder to fall straight into the manger. In the old days the region would be cut off from the rest of the country for weeks and sometimes months at a time, and the winter would be spent in a single room whose main point of attraction was inevitably the fireplace. The monumental bed was occupied by three genera-tions, who were only separated by wooden parti-tions. Benches were set on either side of the long table which had a deep drawer to hold the bread. Another important feature was the sideboard, with four doors, soberly decorated and the pride of the family. Today there is no longer the limitation of the single fireplace and in most of these homes the attics have been furnished and made into extra rooms for the children.

These peasants of the Dordogne have added a little red wine to their last spoonful of soup: an old custom, said to provide extra strength for work. The region is the home of great cooks, and of the truffle mushroom and the confit d'oie *– goose preserved in its own fat.*

A farmer's wife in the chimney corner. Through the long winter months in the Cantal region the grandmother would sit here knitting, and if she had to move would carry about a footwarmer filled with hot ash and cinders.
The chimney corner was also the place to keep the salt.

This elderly guide in Chamonix represents a tradition going back to 1786, when a local man accompanied Michel Paccard on the first ascent of Mont Blanc.

The bread box was originally a plain chest with slatted sides for storing bread, but it evolved into an elaborately carved object. It stood on the kneading trough.

The fruits of the earth

Compared to the north, the southlands are barely industrialised, except round the big cities, along the banks of the Rhône or in the wide valleys of Savoy. Except in the mountain regions and the very dry areas, the land produces food in abundance, although the natural conditions are not always as encouraging as those in the north. In the Roussillon region the inhabitants have had to adapt to a pebbly soil and put up hedges as protection against the constant wind. In the lower Rhône they have had to deal with water hazards. As early as the 18th century canals were dug to irrigate the gardens of La Crau and the Comtat. Today the departments of Hérault and Gard are artificially irrigated by the waters of the Rhône, the

Wood-packing in the Pyrenees, where a flavour of the Middle Ages clings to the mountain passes between France and Spain. These are well watered and thickly wooded, mainly with beech and pine. Trees as high as a ten-storey building brood over thick carpets of fern and dripping moss.

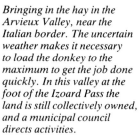

Bringing in the hay in the Arvieux Valley, near the Italian border. The uncertain weather makes it necessary to load the donkey to the maximum to get the job done quickly. In this valley at the foot of the Izoard Pass the land is still collectively owned, and a municipal council directs activities.

The mill at Feliceto in Corsica still crushes the olives by an age-old method. Traditional farming has become unprofitable, and many fields have been left to return to the wild, while bushes and brambles cover many abandoned buildings.

Hérault and the Orb. Growers in the plains and valleys leave the task of watching the heavens for a promise of rain to the men of the hills.

Most of the peasants south of the Loire are smallholders, working as families or using seasonal labour, especially for fruit and vegetable picking. Varying their crops according to the market, they try to predict future changes in prices to make a living. On land suitable for cereals the peasants have a choice between sunflowers, rape seed, sorghum, wheat and sweetcorn or maize. Sweetcorn, a native of the New World, was introduced into the South as early as the 16th century and helped to avert many disasters before the Revolution of 1789 for, unlike wheat, it was not requisitioned in times of famine and was not taxed. It provided food for people as well as animals and is still used to fatten geese and ducks.

In the plains of the Garonne, the Gard and Vaucluse, traditional crops have often been replaced by fruit and vegetables which are considered to be more profitable. In the Roussillon region, soft fruits follow each other from April to October. First come strawberries and cherries. Then, starting in the first week in June, the juicy red apricots, a speciality of the area, are ready. The peaches ripen from May to September, while from July to the end of October the grapes are picked.

Where it is not possible to produce cereals, fruit or vegetables, native 'crops' remain – walnuts from Corrèze and the Dordogne, chestnuts from the Cévennes and truffles from Périgord. This underground mushroom grows best in chalky clay soil, on the roots of common or Turkey oaks, nut trees or limes. As man's sense of smell is not sufficiently developed, specially trained dogs or pigs, which are very fond of the delicacy, are used to sniff it out. The rarity of truffles and the difficulties of collection explain their high price.

Tobacco too is grown in the south. The first seeds were planted in 1637 on the banks of the River Lot where, sheltered from the winds, they flourished on the clay slopes and alluvial plains. Tobacco needs careful cultivation and the grower and his family have to go through many processes – transplanting, banking up, stopping, picking and sorting the leaves one by one – but it brings in an assured income, for the price is guaranteed by the government.

More fragrant – and not such a threat to health – is the flower-growing industry situated between Toulon and Menton in Provence. The flowers grown for their perfume – roses, jasmine, orange blossom and violets – are concentrated around Grasse. The impoverished soils of upper Provence and upper Quercy are suitable for lavender, which makes an important contribution to the income of the inhabitants of these relatively poor areas.

When the few hectares cultivated by an individual family are not enough to feed them, one or more of the members must look for a second job, which is why a grower will work part-time in a local factory, become a municipal employee or possibly an assistant nurse in a hospital – unless he is forced to register as unemployed. The more enterprising will run a business to add to their farming income, the profits going towards buying more land or

modernising their equipment. Others go in for battery farming, which is more profitable. However, after generations of emigration to the north, a change is overtaking the south. During the 1970s many young ecologists left Paris, Lille and other northern cities to raise sheep in the Causses region or in the Cévennes mountains. These experiments were not always very successful but they have sometimes given new inspiration to the locals, who have enough knowledge of the terrain to make the new ideas a viable proposition.

The God-given vine

Whatever the changes that have affected the South its symbol remains the grape, originally introduced by the Romans. The first vines were planted around Narbonne in the 1st century BC and they thrive on the soil of the Languedoc, concentrated in the narrow coastal strip just behind the ultra-modern seaside resorts and clothing the south-facing slopes. In an age of microseconds and fax machines, the vine dictates a less frenetic way of life for its cultivators. In winter the shoots must be pruned, some burned on the spot and others sold in summer to the resort

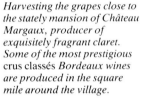

Harvesting the grapes close to the stately mansion of Château Margaux, producer of exquisitely fragrant claret. Some of the most prestigious crus classés Bordeaux wines are produced in the square mile around the village.

shops to be used as fuel for barbecues. In the spring the plants are fumigated and sprayed, using pressure pumps carried on the back or sometimes with the help of helicopters. In September the grapes are harvested and, until harvesting machines become universal, a large labour force has to be employed. Pickers and basket carriers, often from neighbouring Spain, swarm through the vineyards.

The grapes are sent to neighbouring co-operatives, an important feature of village life in the Languedoc and Roussillon, for nowadays very few growers make their own wine. In the department of Hérault around Montpellier, there are 160 co-operatives producing two thirds of the annual national quota. Producers make every effort to improve the quality in order to compete with imported products, particularly as they are now facing competition from Spain within the European Community. However, over-production, nowadays known as the 'wine lake' of the Community, was already a problem in the days of the Romans. An edict issued by the Emperor Domitian in the 1st century limited new plantations in the area because the wines of Narbonne were threatening the native Italian product.

Customs and traditions show the importance that wine has for its producers. In Beaujolais, on the Sunday before the harvest begins, the finest bunches are picked and blessed and then hung up and kept in the house until the end of the harvest as talismans guaranteeing the excellence of the wine. Around Bordeaux, the growers label their wines like aristo-crats who can only live in a castle: Château d'Yquem, Château Margaux, Château Lafite.

Growers jealously guard the quality of the wine which is exported to every country in the world. Twice a year, the members of the Wine Growers' Association of St Emilion meet in the local church, built out of the living rock. The jury, headed by the Grand Master, wear long scarlet gowns and round silk hats. In the spring they judge the new wine and classify the different vintages; in autumn they open the harvest with a solemn proclamation: 'Send your workers in among the vines. May your labours and endeavours be crowned with success.'

In the Armagnac region the grower will admit that he is married to his vines. His life is dedicated to their service: a good Armagnac deserves no less. He must distill it himself and watch over the long maturing process in oak casks, allowing it to take on the golden tinge of the tannin in the wood.

In spite of the introduction of new materials, wood

Cognac tasting requires long training. The famous brandies come from the little town that bears its name, where roofs are blackened by fungus that lives off its fumes. Cognac is wine that is warmed, then twice distilled, then aged in oak casks for at least two years. The best cognacs, labelled VSOP, must be aged at least five years.

Wine-making sustains many ancient crafts, and natural materials need to be used throughout the production cycle. The craft of this cooper of Pauillac, home of some of the finest Bordeaux wines, dates back to the days before the Romans introduced vines into the area and requires great skill. Oak is the best wood to use, particularly if it is fine and close-grained, since it will be rich in tannin. For variety the cooper will use stave-wood from Limousin, between six and ten years old.

remains the best partner of wines and spirits. Wine growing and its traditions have guaranteed the continuance of some trades which might otherwise have disappeared, so coopers continue to practice their craft, handed down to them by the ancient Gauls, producing barrels from oak staves that have matured for at least six years.

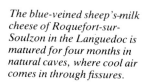

Black truffles from the Périgord are one of the great delicacies of France. Here a customer smells truffles on a market stand to determine their quality.

The blue-veined sheep's-milk cheese of Roquefort-sur-Soulzon in the Languedoc is matured for four months in natural caves, where cool air comes in through fissures.

Salting hams. In some regions the produce is still processed in the traditional way, by hand. Pork, in every possible form, is a prominent feature of French gastronomy.

Where fairs are still held

Ancient market halls still stand in many towns and villages of the South, much admired by tourists, but frequently empty and abandoned. However, the proliferation of supermarkets has not entirely destroyed local traditions. In many parts of the country the peasants still go to town freshly shaved, wearing their Sunday best. They are delighted to meet old friends, exchange the latest gossip and move outside the limited world of their own farm. Although life in the country has become far less isolated, thanks to the telephone and motor car, work on the land is still demanding. Besides, there are so many forms to be filled in to satisfy Paris and Brussels.

Of course, the biggest towns do not necessarily have the best markets. Laguisole, in the department of Aveyron, has a population of only 1200 yet every Thursday crowds pour in from the surrounding countryside and more than a thousand head of cattle are sold. In the Abrac, you have to get up early. The cattlemen and their animals start arriving at the market place from 3 am onwards; sales begin between 5.30 and 6 am and finish at midday. Afterwards

everyone customarily adjourns to the various cafés in the town.

From November to March the sales of foie gras (fattened goose liver) are held in Gascony and the Dordogne. In some districts it is sold by weight; in others they haggle over the quality. This requires more knowledge, but it does give the buyer the opportunity to get the best liver available. Sales are very quick: in a few moments more than a hundredweight of the delicacy can be sold. On the big goose and duck farms, a mechanical fattener has replaced the farmer's wife's traditional hand-operated methods.

Other fairs only take place at certain fixed times of the year. At Eauze, the sales of Armagnac are held during Ascension week. At Gujan-Nestris, in the bay of Arcachon near to Bordeaux, oysters are sold in August. In Agen, halfway between Toulouse and Bordeaux, it is the turn of the plums in the second week of September. At Aubusson in the Limousin region, the *boudins* (sausages) are offered in the same month. The big international fairs in the main towns of the south, Marseilles, Lyons, Bordeaux and Toulouse, are very different events and are far more impersonal.

South of the Loire, as in the north, fast food outlets have appeared in some towns, but countless restaurants continue to flourish, particularly around Lyons and Toulouse, and maintain the tradition of French cuisine. In the countryside, hospitality is still

At Riez, in Provence, the traditional Moustiers pottery is still made using centuries-old methods. An Italian monk is said to have imparted the secret of the blue-white glaze, decorated with shades of blue. Potteries such as this one run by the Clérissy family fit perfectly into the households.

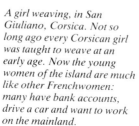

A girl weaving, in San Giuliano, Corsica. Not so long ago every Corsican girl was taught to weave at an early age. Now the young women of the island are much like other Frenchwomen: many have bank accounts, drive a car and want to work on the mainland.

a fine art. Any passing visitor – even the postman bringing a registered letter – will be offered a small glass of something which it is impolite to refuse, even if tea or coffee or even a glass of water might be preferred. In Sauterne, Bergerac or the Jura, you might be offered a liqueur-like drink, or an aperitif from Thuir or Rivesaltes, or a pastis, the aniseed-flavoured clear liquid which turns cloudy when water is added, or fruit in brandy – home-made by the mistress of the house. If she invites you to dinner, often described as supper, she will use her skill to produce the local speciality for which the recipe has been handed down from mother to daughter. If she comes from the Auvergne, it may be a *potée*, a stew with meat and vegetables. If she is from the Limousin she will cook her chicken in butter, with just the right amount of garlic. If she is from Provence she might produce stuffed artichokes. If she is from Languedoc, she could well spend hours simmering the *cassoulet* – a mixture of pork, goose and beans. If she is from Gascony, her speciality will be an apple tart with golden pastry that melts in the mouth. In Périgord, she will produce kid, stewed with wild mushrooms picked and dried the previous autumn. And everything will be served with a smile.

Offsetting this image of hospitality, some places do not have a welcoming reputation. The people of Lyons are often accused of being unwilling to accept newcomers. In the Auvergne they are supposed to be miserly; in the Dauphiné they are suspicious. The only generalisation that can usually be made is that where nature has shown itself kind, where the struggle for existence is not too intense, people are more friendly.

In the old days, the more enterprising men from the Auvergne or Savoy moved to the south-west or to Paris. They opened small shops, selling butter, eggs and cheese, or coffee, wood and coal. As for the Basques, thanks to their energy and adaptability, many of them made fortunes in the Americas, south as well as north, and some returned to their native land and built luxury homes.

Basque clothes are bold and simple; the most characteristic feature, the beret, has become a world favourite. Despite much research, the origins of the Basque people (there are about 200,000 in the south of France) remain a mystery. They have carefully preserved their language, costumes and dances, which may have come from the East.

This costume, brought out at the beginning of summer, is from the plateau of the Rouergue, a rugged region sometimes cut off in winter.

In Arles, where Gauguin and Van Gogh painted, pretty Provençal girls under parasols still thrill to the course à la cocarde, in which daring young men pluck the cocarde, a kind of wreath, from the horns of a charging bull.

Cathars and troubadours

Among the people of the South, certain images of the past still remain vivid. During the 12th century the Cathar sect, which believed that the world had been created by the Devil and that salvation could only be achieved through self-denial, became established in the town of Albi, north-east of Toulouse. At first the Catholic Church tolerated the new movement but, at a time of widespread clerical dissipation, its enormous success came to be seen as a threat. In 1208 Pope Innocent III appointed Simon de Montfort leader of a crusade against the sect that had come to be known as the Albigensians. However, the crusade was not just a matter of religious intolerance. The invaders were also irresistibly attracted by the wealth of the South. Toulouse, Montpellier, Albi, Foix and Carcassonne were at that time brilliant centres of civilisation, unfettered by allegiance to the French crown and inheritors of a Greco-Roman culture that was under the Moorish-Arab influence that had crossed the Pyrenees from Spain.

In 1213 de Montfort defeated Raymond VI, Count of Toulouse at Muret and let his troops loose on the towns and cities of the region. The slaughter was largely indiscriminate, nearly half the victims being children. Despite de Montfort's death at the hands of a Toulousain stonemason, the persecution continued. For ten years the citadel of Montségur became the centre of resistance. When it surrendered in 1244, its unworldly inhabitants chose to be burned alive rather than deny their faith. Although the kings of France nominally controlled the region, the wild terrain protected those who worshipped in secret and when Calvinism, another call to self-denial, spread across France in the 16th century it took hold in the old Albigensian strongholds. This eventually led to more blood-letting in the religious wars of the 16th and 17th centuries, and the hostility between Protestants and Catholics persisted well into the 19th century. Every summer the town of Albi remembers its past persecution in a magnificent son et lumière.

The troubadours, of whom the first known was William, grandfather of the energetic Eleanor of Aquitaine, originated in the Midi in the 11th century. These aristocratic song writers and poets addressed love songs to the wives of local lords whose marriages were affairs of politics not of affection. They were also the forerunners of literary satirists and modern lyricists who used their positions at court to criticise the manners of the day and the politics of the great. The beauty of their work was an inspiration to many 19th-century French writers.

The typical Auvergne man is hard-working, thrifty and patient as he works the volcanic soil in this region of starkly geometric mountains. Auvergne men still 'go up to Paris' to become wine merchants, furniture dealers, civil servants, or even – and it has happened – presidents of France.

Having a good time

Today the people of the Midi seem to be looking in two directions at the same time: towards the 11th and the 21st centuries. The young families of Grenoble and Toulouse look towards a future created by the technologically orientated, fast-growing companies that have become an established feature of the South. In summer the Midi is awash with tourists who come for the sunshine and the sea, of course, but also for the past – Roman ruins, the 11th- and 12th-century Romanesque churches, the Gothic cathedrals, the châteaux and the fortified towns.

Meanwhile, in the small towns the flower markets are thriving; fishermen return at dawn from lamp-lit all-night sessions; players argue hotly over a few centimetres of dusty ground at the climax of their game of boules; cafés serve glasses of *pastis*, with loud voices raised in the accents made famous by the playwright Marcel Pagnol, making fun of Parisians or roundly criticising the government of the day.

Then there are the festivals. The carnival in Nice and its parade of decorated cars is the most famous but there are also others, like the one held in Pézenas in the department of Hérault. The town's heyday was in the 17th century, and some magnificent old houses have survived from this period. When the carnival starts on Monday evening the streets are filled with extraordinary figures – the *soufflaculs* – fantastically dressed dancers who start with the 'dance of the soufflets' by extending paper whistles which they point at their neighbour's backside and blow. The next morning, Shrove Tuesday, a pony is led in procession through the city, followed by great crowds.

After carnival time there is a lull until Easter. In Sartène, Corsica, the Good Friday procession arouses intense fervour and is conducted with a pomp reminiscent of the Middle Ages. The procession is headed by the *catenac-ciù*, the 'great penitent', who carries the cross. Barefoot and wearing a red robe and hood so as not to be recognised, he follows the steep road to the setting symbolic of Calvary with a heavy chain fastened round his legs, endeavouring to expiate his sins or even a crime. Behind him, black-robed penitents carry an impressive carving of the dead Christ.

An equally emotional atmosphere is created around the procession of the Black Virgin of Le Puy in the department of the Haute-Loire. This cult may date from pre-Christian days since the cathedral of Notre-Dame, which is built on the top of the huge Corneille rock, replaced a Roman temple. The bull running, which takes place in the Basque country and throughout Provence, probably came from Spain but may well be another legacy from an ancient cult.

Bulls are also at the centre of the 'rosette' contests, in which the animal is brought to the centre of the arena and the contestant must snatch the rosette fastened between the bull's horns. Any form of acrobatics is allowed in order to avoid being gored.

In these celebrations there is as much variation as there is between other aspects of life in the Midi. In the land of sunshine, traditions are alive and well and although the people of the South have a culture that stretches 2000 years into the past, their future is in enterprising hands. From Grenoble in the east to Bordeaux in the west, the land of the Midi is a land on the move.

Even on a calm day in the bay of Porto, there is a sense of drama about life in Corsica, where the people are known for the passion with which they have waged vendettas, or taken to the maquis – the bush – as outlaws whenever some law displeased them. Napoleon was a Corsican, and believed the island 'better and more beautiful than anywhere else'.

Belgium

This triangle of land wedged between Germanic and Latin worlds,
with a window onto the North Sea, is a divided land. There is such a split
between its language-based communities, and such sensitivity, that it is
proper to insist that there is no king of Belgium, but only a king of the
Belgians. Constantly pillaged, and in its time forcibly linked to Spain, to
Austria, to France and to the Netherlands, Belgium has existed as a nation
only since 1830. But now it is finding itself as it brings together
old enemies and provides a capital for the new Europe.

Numerous ferries link England with Belgium. Several times a day, the boats from Dover and Harwich tie up at Ostend's long wooden jetty. Crusaders set out from here, and so did pirates; more recently, it was a resort for European royalty.

Antwerp's mighty port is one of the world's most efficient, handling 17,000 ships from 100 countries every year. The city's commercial activities are augmented by a great cultural tradition.

Previous page: *Three ladies of Blankenberge in their Flemish finery. Former fishing villages that have become fashionable summer resorts are careful to preserve their customs, and hold out against the encroaching concrete.*

The Cockpit of Europe

The extraordinary thing about these people who have been conquered over and over again is that the Belgians still exist. Julius Caesar called them the 'bravest of the brave', and the statue of Ambiorix, hero of the struggle against the Romans (led personally by Caesar), stands in the middle of the market square at Tongeren, where in 54 BC he rallied the tribes. Belgium has had need of many statues to honour heroes of this sort, but perhaps the best symbol of its spirit of resistance to adversity and defiance against poverty is in the painting by Brueghel the Elder of *Dulle Griet* (Mad Margaret), the helmeted mad-woman personifying war, or in his *Peasants' Dance*, showing the joyous abandon which was long considered the cure for all ills.

With few natural defences, the Low Countries, and especially the part that is now Belgium, suffered so much from invasion that it became known as the Cockpit of Europe; even today, NATO's defence of western Europe is based upon unrestricted access to the same ports that have been the objective of armies down the ages. Belgium is not naturally rich or fertile, and it has taken many generations of peasant toil to make it productive. The climate is similar to that of Britain, though slightly colder and damper – it is said to rain on more than 200 days in the year.

It takes two hours to drive across Belgium from east to west, and four hours to drive from north to south. From the air practically the whole country can be surveyed at a single glance. Nearly 10 million people live within a territory that measures 200 miles by 100 miles at its widest points, and from the flat coastland to the hills of the Ardennes it swarms with activity. It begins as a strip of North Sea beach pounded by grey-white rollers. Offshore, the little boats dance on the foam, while sand-yachts, invented here 300 years ago to amuse a prince, race over the hard sand. Halfway along the coast is the jutting jetty of Ostend (Oostende), fussed over by the ferries from Dover and Folkestone, while mussel and smoked mackerel sellers shelter from the wind behind their canvas stalls. Close to the beach, for the 40 miles from De Panne, on the French border, to Knokke on the Dutch border, cliffs of flats and hotels have risen above the former fishing villages of Koksijde, Westende, Blankenberge and Zeebrugge, distinguishable only by the place names on the bus stops – or you can take a tram ride all the way from border to border.

Behind this concrete strip lies Flanders, its diked and poldered water meadows dotted with great white farmhouses, and patrolled by long lines of poplars bent by the wind from the sea. The poplars mark the course of canals, and of roads linking villages, which you can count by their church spires. The wealth of this region has been built up slowly and painstakingly, through centuries of carefully cultivating the poor sandy soil and planting it with towns like Bruges (Brugge), Ypres, Courtrai, Ghent (Gent), Malines and Antwerp – towns that are among the most striking in Europe.

'God made us Flemish; only politics made us Belgian' – this often-repeated slogan says much about the Flemings, who have not been independent since 1384, yet still have a fierce sense of what it must have been like, and are ever wary of cultural domination. From earliest times their land has been steeped in blood, as anyone who pins on a poppy in November is acknowledging. The story of Ypres, out on the Flemish plain, is a testament to human resilience. The town was already an important cloth centre in Roman times, and its gigantic Cloth Hall, dating from 1214, demonstrates the scale of this industry in medieval times, when Ypres was more than three times the size it is today. But the Cloth Hall, like the cathedral and the rows of 17th-century houses, is a loving reconstruction, for Ypres was obliterated

These crisp biscuits, shaped like 19th-century characters and flavoured with cinnamon and cloves, are a Belgian speciality. Children adore their grotesque shapes, while collectors look on them as creations of popular art. Gaily decorated with ribbons, they are sold in an old building behind the Grand' Place in Brussels.

during the First World War. Around this town that the British troops called 'Wipers', hundreds of thousands of men died in years of mindless trench warfare, and now every evening, beside ancient fortifications that no bombardment could destroy, the traffic stops and a bugler blows the 'Last Post' for those who lie all about.

Flanders is drained by the River Scheldt, which is so laden with silt and barges that it has been called 'a moving road'. The river winds lazily between banks burdened with factories until it reaches the great harbour of Antwerp, where it spreads into a delta of shapeless sandbanks, and white birds and windmills, which at some point are no longer Belgian, but Dutch. The great port of the Middle Ages was Bruges, now left high and almost dry with its memories, for the same storms that choked its harbour opened up the Scheldt.

In the 16th century, when a thousand trading businesses crowded the town, it was said that 'Antwerp owes the Scheldt to God, and everything else to the Scheldt.' It is no less true today. The world's biggest lock, at Zandvliet, enables big ships to enter, and the 741 docking bays reach almost into Dutch territory. Now a road tunnel has been built under the river and attention is turning to the undeveloped left bank, for there are plans to double the size of a port that already handles an annual 85 million tons of goods from 17,000 ships of 100 nationalities. Of Antwerp's population of half a million, one in six works in the docks, which are owned by the town. This makes the dockers

municipal employees and seemingly less prone to militant trade unionism. Antwerp is also where 70 per cent of the world's diamonds change hands. The so-called 'Antwerp quality' gemstones require such skill in cutting and polishing that local specialists are the only ones who dare to undertake the work. The process is so intricate and time-consuming that research is under way to see whether lasers can speed up, or even replace, the traditional methods.

Rape of the black country

Inland from the Scheldt flows the Meuse. Between the rivers is the lonely region known as the Kempen (Campine), with its sandy moorland and scrub, heather and broom, its sheep and skies that artists loved to paint. South again, in the French-speaking province of Hainaut, signs of depression are everywhere as this industrial region struggles against the effects of the decline of the coal and steel industries. Overgrown railway tracks, their points broken, run beside the winding gear of mines that stand idle, with their shafts blocked. 'It's a good wheel that turns,' is a saying hereabouts. This is the Borinage, the black corridor from Mons to Charleroi that is as exhausted as its coal. Legend has it that on August 23, 1914 angels appeared over Mons and rallied British soldiers as they faced a massive German onslaught, but there has been scant evidence of heavenly help since then. It is a ravaged landscape of derelict and abandoned factories, bleak monuments to those who have toiled here since coal was first wrested from the ground in the 13th century.

At Wasmes, in the 'people's house' where the *gueules noires* (coal heads) once relaxed over a jar and a game of cards, a placard propped against a mirror is scrawled with the enigmatic message: 'Like our grandparents in 1886'. An ex-miner's wife, old before her time, explains its meaning. 'In 1886,' she says, 'my grandfather fought for the right to vote. In 1926, my father demanded an increase in wages. He tried again in 1932, and they clapped him in gaol to teach him better manners. In 1950, it was my husband's turn to down tools. In 1961, it started again, because taxes were going up while social security was being cut down . . . and there was worse to come. But what's the use? You can't start tomorrow with yesterday. There's nothing left.'

A canal (here it is the canal from Damme to Bruges) or a road, edged by tall poplars bent by the sea breezes, with a veiled sky filtering a slant of sunlight . . . Flemish painting is rich in works inspired by this vision.

At the heart of the most densely populated corner of Europe, this stretch of the Sambre has been spared from encroaching industry. As for the rivers of the Ardennes, they have kept their natural state and remain the haunt of trout and kingfisher alike.

Such thoughts are commonly expressed behind the spotless curtains of the small working-class homes of the industrial towns: homes that seem to be plunged in an uneasy slumber, now that the factories are silent and the whistles no longer summon the shift-workers at all hours. The artist Van Gogh lived for a time in Wasmes, in a house in woody marshland at the end of a roughly paved road. Not far away in another little house, now almost sunk in reeds and mud, Van Gogh preached the Gospel with fiery zeal, and identified himself so completely with the miners that he came to look like one of them. He lived in poverty, gave away his clothes and nursed typhoid victims, but he was sacked as a troublemaker when he pestered the authorities to improve the miners' miserable lot. At least the outside world benefited, for Van Gogh, released from this obsession, went on to create the magnificent canvases of his few remaining years.

Charleroi, Dinant, Namur, Liège – between the Meuse and the Sambre runs the time-honoured route of invasion, and these two rivers lend their names to a military march that is as familiar to French ears as 'The British Grenadiers' or 'Stars and Stripes' are to British and American ones. Charleroi was held in turn by the Spanish, the French and the Prussians, and by the Germans through both world wars; so was Dinant, which has been pillaged repeatedly since the Romans named it after Diana, goddess of the hunt. Namur, cursed by its strategic site at the junction of the Meuse and Sambre, has been razed regularly in 2000 years of struggle.

Liège is different. This factory city on the Meuse is where much that is best in the Belgian spirit is most in evidence: the spirit of rebellion, and pride in traditional ways. Remarkably for a place so crowded by steelworks and pitheads that it is nicknamed the 'ardent city', it contrives to be beautiful as well, with quaint districts and old churches in the care of many interesting saints, including one adept at curing toothache, and another at providing protection against lightning. The composer César Franck and the novelist Georges Simenon came from Liège, as did any number of gruff and bold characters ready to champion noble causes.

A field of flax near Veurne. Flanders flax, which produces superb linen, has been grown since the days of the Spanish empire, and Veurne remains the most Spanish of Flemish towns, as monuments to the Duke of Alba's rule in the 16th century testify.

A house in Flanders. White walls, with foundations damp-proofed and black paint used decoratively, are characteristic of northern Belgium. There is a sharp contrast between the simplicity of these small homes and the ostentatious, over-decorated style which architects considered appropriate for a business enterprise.

Hops are a common sight in Flanders; they grow on long wooden poles linked by wires. It is the secretion of the seeds, mixed with gums and essences in proportions determined by the brewer, that gives beer its refreshing tang and bitterness.

The face of the Flemish peasant reflects his character. He is a man of dogged determination, unlikely to let himself be imposed upon. The Dutch-speaking Flemish live in the north and the French-speaking Walloons in the south, with Brussels designated a dual-language area.

The history of Liège is one long struggle for individual liberty, with its bishop-princes locked in combat with powerful neighbours, and its fiercely independent citizens in combat with the prince-bishops, until the last was removed during the French Revolution. Thereupon, the Liègeois fought bravely for Belgian independence, and in 1914 they heroically withstood the Germans before the crucial Battle of the Marne.

The cafés of Liège stay open far into the night, and the conversation today is of the woes of steel, and the uncertain fortunes of the Fabrique National-ale, the giant small-arms manufacturer whose FN rifle became a familiar NATO weapon. Arms have been made here for centuries, and now there is a move back to hand-crafted weapons, some of them superbly executed and engraved collector's pieces that cost a million Belgian francs (£15,000) each.

Beyond Liège are the Ardennes: a hilly frontier at last, but rivers cut like sword-strokes through the hills to afford further invasion routes. Here in 1944 was fought the Battle of the Bulge, when the Americans halted the last, desperate thrust of Nazi Germany. During times of peace, when the soldiers left the woods to the wild boars and the deep valleys were left to brood and grow legends, the Ardennes were celebrated for the curative powers of their waters – so much so that health resorts everywhere came, in English, to be named after the Ardennes town of Spa. The springs of Spa were known to the Romans as *Aquae Sepadonae*, and later proved a lure for Peter the Great of Russia and a parade of European royalty. From the 18th century, casinos added to the pleasures of the cure, and Spa achieved an elegance that earned it the title 'Café of Europe'. Today, the aristocracy has departed, to be replaced by the beneficiaries of Belgium's national health scheme, and an ultra-modern plant bottles Spa water for commercial distribution. But if the neighbourhood has lost something in international status the chips are delicious, canoeing is pleasantly peaceful, and visits can be organised to abbeys where the monks, in working towards their own salvation, brew beer strong enough to delight the damned.

The Grand' Place in Brussels has been called the most beautiful square in the world. It is completely surrounded by sumptuously decorated 17th-century guild houses, each with its own emblem (a fox, a wheelbarrow, a mill, a ship), and is dominated by the imposing gothic Hôtel de Ville, or town hall.

Domestic differences

Beer is the national drink, and if the Belgians have sorrows to drown, they have plenty of choice in the matter. While the standardisation of big-scale brewing has led to the domination of a light lager type, there are still about 130 breweries producing more than 400 types of beer, including many local specialities. As well as the strong monastic brews there is a thousand-year-old wheat-based beer called *faro* and a popular wheat-barley beer called *gueuze*; there are frothy beers, golden beers, and even a cherry-flavoured beer called *kriek*. In case this is insufficient choice, imported beers are freely available, and suffcent Belgians have acquired a taste for British bitter for it to be brewed locally. Wine drinkers are equally well provided for. Belgian Meuse vines did not survive the First World War, and an attempt at making wine from the famous Belgian hot-house grapes has had limited success, but the very best French wines have traditionally found their way to Belgium, and even the cheap lines of the supermarkets are of a superior quality.

This best-of-both-worlds is the positive side to Belgium's great and overwhelming dilemma: it is two countries in one. Where Luxembourg and Switzerland mix languages merrily and create unity out of their diversity, Belgium is divided against itself, and in few countries are internal relations harder to manage. Forget for the moment the presence of a pocket of German-speakers wedged against the borders with Luxembourg and western Germany.

For practical purposes there are two Belgian peoples: the Dutch-speaking Flemish in the north and the French-speaking Walloons in the south. They face each other across a line drawn slightly south of the capital, Brussels, and are ever alert to the merest hint of a cultural slight. Brussels itself is designated as bilingual, a sort of neutral zone, even though it is a mainly French-speaking island in Flemish territory; it has evolved its own dialect, a colourful language mix called Bruxellois.

Some experts trace the bickering back to tribal divisions of 1600 years ago, and the Flemings still commemorate a battle of 1302 when their ancestors routed the French. But the real source of sensitivity lies in much more recent times, when French was the language of the ruling class, and Dutch-speakers were underdogs, largely illiterate and consigned to the most menial jobs, and obliged to learn French if they wanted to get ahead. In 1830 Belgium became an independent nation with an uncle of Queen Victoria as king. However, it was not until 1898 that Flemish (the local dialect of Dutch) was accorded equal status with French, and even then the enmity was such that some of the Flemish community welcomed the Germans as liberators in the First World War. As inter-community relations worsened, the economic

Brussels bustles with small markets at weekends. Bird-lovers meet behind the Grand' Place; antique fairs are set up behind the Place des Sablons; arts and crafts flourish in the surrounding alleys. The flea markets are mostly in the poorer Marolles district.

A flower-market is set up daily in the Grand' Place, which the municipality sometimes fills with begonias to turn the square into a Persian carpet.

balance began to swing from south to north with the Great Depression; this process accelerated with the collapse of the southern coal and steel industries, and a northern resurgence in agriculture and light industry, after the Second World War. Now it was the turn of the Walloons to fear Flemish domination, particularly since a faster Flemish birthrate had given them a clear numerical superiority. Secession by the south was canvassed for a time, and in 1962 an internal border, the 'Language Frontier', was drawn between the two communities. This was followed in 1980 by a new federal constitution of extraordinary complexity, the aim being to create a fully bi-cultural country, with a lot of the power being divested among the regions.

The Belgian nation is today a wary alliance of 5.5 million Flemish and 3 million Walloons, who are determined to avoid domination of any kind. A consequence of this is so much bureaucratic duplication that Belgium must have the highest proportion of officials anywhere. Apart from the central government with its built-in Flemish majority in the House of Deputies and the Senate, there is a Walloon assembly in Namur, and twin law courts, one Walloon and the other Flemish, both sit in Brussels. Not to be left out, the 66,000 German-speaking Belgians also have their own communal authorities, and, naturally, each community has to have its own executive body. As for Brussels, no one has been able to decide on its future, so its direction is left to three ministers from the central government. Brussels, the big prize, in a way holds the country together, for neither community would ever consider letting go of it.

Consider also the cross-cultural division between Catholic traditionalist and anti-clerical Socialist, and it is hardly surprising that such a complexity of competing authorities and interests should sometimes be the cause of violent dispute. The answer is the *compromis à la belge*, a way of fudging issues and avoiding any decision that is going to antagonise one side or the other. The populace is assured at every election that 'the traditional good sense of the Belgians will always win through', but so fragile are the coalitions, and so recurrent are government crises, that solutions can always be put off to an eternal tomorrow, and legislation that is sometimes as incomprehensible as it is complicated continues to be enacted, if not always enforced. Fondly remembered is the comment of a former Prime Minister, Camille Huysman, on the text of one particular law: 'When it was drawn up, two of us knew what it meant – God and myself. But now, I have forgotten.' What happened at Louvain, the ancient and great university of Erasmus, illustrates the depth of feeling.

The university was bilingual, even though it is in Flanders, and this so incensed Flemish students, who had no wish to tolerate their francophone (French-speaking) companions, that in 1970 a twin university, Louvain-la-Neuve, was created by the authorities in Walloon territory especially for French-speakers.

The big dilemma for the visitor is knowing which language to use, for the wrong choice can cost a relationship, or a business deal. Names are no more of a guide than looks, for intermarriage has obscured much of the difference between the shorter, darker, more volatile Walloon and the taller, fairer, dour Fleming, and the most Flemish-sounding name can conceal a francophone and vice versa. The best advice is never to open a conversation in French in the Flemish part of the country.

Arcades (this one is the Galerie du Roi) are a feature of Brussels, which is justly famous for its shops. Elegant boutiques and their cosmopolitan clientele fit very well into the period setting.

Almost three-quarters of the world's diamonds pass through the hands of Antwerp merchants. Only a small proportion will become gemstones, after a cutting process so delicate that research is being carried out to see if it can be done by laser.

The consumption of chips – frites – in Belgium is enormous. They are part of the daily diet, with considerable increases on the many public holidays. Pretty girls don't seem unduly worried by warnings of the dangers of over-indulgence.

Capital of Europe

The extent of Belgium's success in covering over its cracks is evident in the image it now presents to the outside world. In seeking to diffuse domestic dispute, it looked outwards and was an early promoter of European unity. First through the Benelux customs union with the Netherlands and Luxembourg, then through NATO and the European Community, it came to be a focus of international activity, and in this way Brussels found itself 'Capital of Europe', the boomtown of the Eurocrats.

The old streets of Brussels are named after the businesses that once traded there: butchers and brewers, cheesemongers and fishmongers, hatters and steam-pressers. In the heart of the city, behind the theatrical setting of the fashionable cafés set around the Grand' Place, 31 rue au Beurre (Butter Street) is typical of the establishments to be found there. Two-storeyed, and built of brick with stone balconies, it has tall windows filled with small leaded panes of glass. The shop on the ground floor is the Maison Dandoy, which since 1829 has been selling macaroons, cakes, sweets, chocolates and crisp cinnamon-flavoured biscuits tied with ribbons, shaped like toy soldiers, Father Christmases, or small animals; called *speculaus*, these are designed for elegant nibbling, in contrast to the huge, well-filled

rolls called *pistolets*, which are a meal in themselves. A tiny staircase, steep as a ladder, ascends into the darkness, to upper floors where the private lives of the proprietors have to be imagined.

In such surroundings, it is easy to sense the continuity of a city whose Hôtel de Ville (Town Hall) dates from 1422, and whose origins can be traced back to 966 and the reign of Otto the Great, when it was known as Brocsella (from *broeck*, meaning marsh, and *sali*, a dwelling). A few paces from Dandoy's the architecture breaks into a riot of curving balconies, ramps and doorways, for here is where, in the late 19th century, art nouveau architecture was born and brought fame to its creator, the Belgian architect Victor Horta. Alas, movements more momentous than this have now overtaken the city, and whole districts have been disembowelled for the creation of expressways. Brussels has required extensive remodelling to carry the infrastructure of the European Community, whose language is the moneyspeak of finance, and whose buildings look exactly like enormous banks; indeed, the huge, four-pronged Berlaymont building, leased by Belgium to the European Commission, is owned by an international bank.

An astronomical rise in the cost of living, due in part to the legendary expense accounts of the Eurocrats, has put many citizens to flight, and not all of

The wild boar of the Ardennes maintains its reputation for savagery, but its ham is delectable when smoked over sweet-smelling gorse branches. The Ardennes is a region of forests and villages, with memorials to recall that here was fought the Battle of the Bulge in the Second World War.

The industrialisation of Charleroi extends deep into the black, slag-heaped heart of the Borinage region, and is the most forbidding aspect of Belgium. Despite official optimism, attempts at reversing the decay in the country's central coal basin have not convinced the miners that better times are just around the corner. Conducted tours in glass-topped boats on the Brussels-Charleroi Canal so that tourists can admire a view 'unique in Europe', does not solve the problem.

It only takes a little colour to transform a sombre urban setting. Against the prevailing grey, white is an essential element of a palette in which each flower has an opportunity to glow.

those who remain are delighted with their changed city. Chez Toone is one of the little *estaminets* (a word for 'bar' left behind by the Spanish) where friendships quickly spring up, and this one is special, for it is among the last where the wooden marionettes (Toones) from the 17th century still give nightly, biting comments on current events. Here over a beer a man can become melancholy about the passing of old ways, yet there remain cobbled corners, old canals, flea markets and more than a whiff of the atmosphere that Brueghel depicted when he lived here 400 years ago.

Good food, and plenty of it

Not that the soul of the citizen has changed. That Brussels has more restaurants per head than Paris has more to do with Belgian ways than with the gluttony of Eurocrats. Eating is a favourite Belgian pastime – they like good food and plenty of it – but Belgians like to keep their home life private, so even close friends often prefer to entertain one another in a restaurant.

In the Ardennes, where living conditions can be very basic, the farming community forms a closed world that is very hard to penetrate. Something of the wild boar lurking in the undergrowth has rubbed off on the people, and it takes years to get to know

them. While city dwellers are a lot more forth-coming, there comes a point where they also prefer to retreat behind closed doors. And closed windows, too: in what seems to be an over-reaction to the climate, homes tend to be over-heated in winter, and even in summer the curtains are likely to be drawn and windows closed, for Belgians seem to have a morbid fear of draughts. Since family ties are very important and take precedence over other relation-ships, it follows that it is not easy to strike up friendships with Belgians, and it takes a long time for an acquaintance to be invited into a Belgian home. Parents in particular try to spend as much time as possible at home, so lunchtimes are their best oppor-tunity to meet friends and relations or see a play or

concert, and entertainment in Brussels is planned with this in mind. This respectable way of life is supported by a large and vigilant police force; no hippies, please – they can take themselves off to Amsterdam or Copenhagen. Women move about freely, with no fear of being molested wherever they go, though 'liberation' is not an issue high on the Belgian agenda.

The Catholic Church remains a major influence on a society that is overwhelmingly conservative and so middle-class that there is even a government Minister for the Middle Classes. Christian names are not for casual use, and people are addressed as *Monsieur* and *Madame*, or *Mijn Heer* and *Mevrouw*, far longer than would be the case in most other countries. A lot of formalised greeting goes on, and even children expect a hand-shake. Most young people tend to live at home until they get married, and many students studying away from home will invariably return to their parents at the weekends. Money and material wealth is a supreme consideration, and the legend of fortunes kept in woollen socks, or under the

Bruges, the silted-up 'Venice of the North', is the most complete medieval town in northern Europe. Reflected in its dark canals are memories of its merchant princes, of St Ursula, Charles the Bold and Philip the Good. Its many treasures range from a gold reliquary, said to contain drops of the blood of Christ, to masterpieces by Hans Memling, Jan van Eyck and Hieronymus Bosch.

The lacemakers' shops are survivors of an industry which contributed much to the wealth of Bruges, and illustrate the city's capacity to make time stand still – and to turn it to touristic effect.

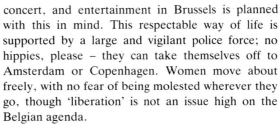

A great seaport in the Middle Ages, Bruges is now stranded 14 miles inland, yet its network of canals gives it the feel of an island. Tourist boats navigate through a labyrinth of greenery and flower-decked balconies to land their cargoes on the terrace of a delightful hotel.

mattress, is still very much alive. Possession of property is the main measure of success; a farmer may possess 125 acres and not have a bathroom. He may live like a poor man without being one.

These are characteristics developed through generations of adversity and occupation, and so is the Belgians' great tolerance of strangers, so long as they do not interfere with them or with their way of life. This 'live and let live' attitude has also produced a suspicion of authority and a lack of discipline – in queueing, for instance – and also what can appear as a certain rudeness – Belgian drivers are notorious. Nor is punctuality the rule. Except for doctors' or dentists' appointments, it is usual to the point of being customary to arrive late, and it follows that public performances rarely start on time.

Belgians have a great zest for life. No people enjoy a celebration more, and if they prize material things, they demand the best, so the shops and supermarkets are stocked with a variety and quality of goods superior to that in most other countries. Service is also excellent, and gift wrapping an art.

On any fine weekend, everybody rushes either to the coast or to the Ardennes, causing a traffic jam the length of the nation, and occasions like weddings are celebrated in high style, usually with a big restaurant meal to conclude, for good eating is a particular joy in a country where cholesterol seems to hold no perils. Think of Belgian chocolates, especially the hand-made, cream-filled pralines, which are the best in the world.

Materialism has its benefits, and the princes and rich merchants who supported great Flemish artists like Memling, the Brueghels and Rubens, have been replaced by banks, businesses and the state, so young artists and poets flourish, and galleries thrive, with the public ready to invest in new works and new styles in a way quite at odds with their normal conservatism; one result, perhaps most appropriate to Belgium, was the popularity of the surrealism of René Magritte and others.

Toones are large stick puppets dating back to the 17th century, when the theatre was the preserve of the rich and puppets provided entertainment for the common folk. Events were commented upon in the bluntest manner, leading to brisk exchanges between puppeteer and spectator. This method of airing grievances can still be enjoyed in Brussels, Antwerp and Liège.

These youngsters dressing up as a character known as 'Gilles' are armed and ready for the Carnival of Binche (in the south of Belgium) in which there is an orgy of orange throwing. The wild celebration, in which thousands of marchers wear costumes hung with bells and tall plumed hats, is thought to stem from an Inca dance brought back by the Spanish when they conquered Peru.

Luxembourg

'We want to remain what we are' is the deeply-felt national motto
of the 378,000 citizens of the Grand Duchy, and it is carved and painted on
buildings throughout their 999 square miles of domain, squeezed between
Belgium, Germany and France. The Grand Duchy has provided four Holy
Roman Emperors, four kings of Bohemia and a king of Hungary in the course
of its thousand-year history. In recent times, declarations of neutrality
did not prevent it from suffering two German occupations, so now it follows
a policy of very active participation in the European Community.
It is a constitutional monarchy with power in the hands of
an elected Chamber of Deputies, and an immensely popular royal family
headed by the Grand Duke Jean, a thoroughly modern monarch
trained in law and political science.

The little town of Echternach carefully preserves its past and seems to embody the Luxembourgers' slogan: 'We wish to remain what we are'. As if to stress the point, Echternach stands on the banks of the River Sûre, the frontier with Germany.

Previous page: The old wine presses of Bech-Kleinacher, one of the many villages of the Luxembourg Moselle region; its museum in an 18th-century house traces the region's long wine-making tradition.

The Springprozession at Echternach honours Willibrord, a saint from Northumberland who founded the abbey here in 698. The procession takes the form of a jerky dance – five hops forward, then three back – by pilgrims linked by twisted handkerchiefs. It dates back to the Middle Ages, when it was thought to cure epilepsy.

Prudent Lilliput

Before the Second World War, Luxembourg was best known to the British as a broadcasting station which relayed popular recorded music in the evening, when the BBC confined itself to palm court orchestras. Today it is one of the headquarters of the European Community, and this has helped draw attention to its delightful countryside and towns. There is picturesque Echternach, for instance, where they still revere an English saint called Willibrord, hardly known in England, who brought them the gospel 1300 years ago. In the capital's cathedral lie the remains of blind King John who, despite his disability, fought against and so impressed the English at the Battle of Crécy that his three feathers and motto *Ich Dien* (I serve) have been used ever since as the arms of the Prince of Wales.

The tiny country contains three distinct 'regions'. The mountainous Ardennes, full of castles and forests, descends from the Belgian frontier in the north to the Gutland ('good lands') of rolling, rich farmlands, which in turn stretches southwards to the tall chimneys of the steel plants and to the vineyards of the Mosel which, a 20-minute drive from the capital, forms the border with Germany.

The fine houses, with perfectly maintained façades, reflect the people of Echternach's pride in a town that is soon to celebrate its 1300th birthday.

'Holy Willibrord, founder of churches, light of the blind, destroyer of idols, pray for us . . . .' To this repeated chant, and the clamour of bands, the pilgrims set forth at the toll of a seven-ton bell; they take all morning to reach the basilica, where the bones of the saint lie. Once blessed, the pilgrims become revellers, and much Moselle wine is drunk long into the night.

The nationals of the Grand Duchy are not plagued by the linguistic divisions of their Belgian neighbours. They all speak some Letzeburghish, an ancient Franco-Mosel dialect with French and German additions, which is acquired from the cradle. They are taught German and French in primary school, have the option of adding Spanish in secondary school, and generally learn English as well. Newspapers and the political and cultural worlds operate on bilingual Franco-German lines, so, at the very least, the country can claim to be trilingual.

Cautious and level-headed, the Luxembourgers have embraced the concept of a united Europe with enthusiasm, and are benefiting accordingly. While the great driving force behind the economy has been the steel industry, the ever-increasing role that the country is playing in the affairs of the Community is contributing to its achievement of the highest living standards of any member state. The many EC institutions established there have transformed the plateau of Kirchberg into a sprawling city, whose citadels include the steel and glass European Court of Justice, and the 23-storey tower block which houses the Secretariat of the European Parliament; here the Council of Ministers meets three times a year, as part of a process known to Luxembourgers as 'the circus'. So long as no decision is taken on the rival claims of Brussels, Strasbourg and Luxembourg to be its permanent home, the Council sits in each location in turn. This is the explanation for the immense and virtually constant convoy of lorries transporting files, typewriters, word processors, translators and all the other paraphernalia and personnel between the three centres.

Of course, the presence of such an army, together with the 120 foreign banks and 5000 holding companies that have settled in the Duchy, has its compensations. The Luxembourgers maintain a serene detachment as they count their commission and invest some of the proceeds in the conservation of their historic little towns, carefully restoring one fine old castle after another.

It has been said that Luxembourg is less a country than a state of mind. This was never more evident than during the Second World War, when the Nazis over-ran the country within hours, but the royal family and leading politicians escaped to form a government-in-exile, while thousands of young Luxembourgers fled to enlist in all the Allied armies. Those who remained went on strike, and suffered all sorts of reprisals. The war ended with more than half of the roads, 160 bridges and tunnels and the homes of 60,000 people destroyed, and 35 per cent of the farmland so devastated that it could not be tilled. Within ten years, the Grand Duchy had rebounded to such prosperity that Luxembourg's gross national product per capita was the sixth highest in the world, and the highest in Europe. The achievement was made easier by the shared sense of purpose of a simple people, who turned to advantage their strategic position in the heart of western Europe, one which had caused so much havoc in the past.

From Schengen to Wasserbillig, vineyards cover the slopes along the Luxembourg Moselle. They produce a fairly dry white wine, more like Rhine wine than the fruitier French Moselles. There are also sparkling vins mousseux *at less than half the price of similar champagnes, and the pleasing, less fizzy* vins perlés.

The Netherlands

It has been said that a nation is only really civilised
'when it has acquired qualities denied it by nature'. If this is true,
then Holland (the popular name, though strictly speaking it refers to only
two coastal provinces) is the most civilised of nations, for it is the most
unnatural. From the air, it looks like a patchwork quilt that has been
ironed flat, or like a survey map drafted by a mad geometrician:
it looks too perfect, too contrived, to be real. And in a way, it is not real.
By the laws of nature, most of the country should not exist, and these same
laws make most of the country a constant potential disaster area.

Children have always had a special place in Dutch life. Even in the 17th century, foreigners were amazed by the freedom of their behaviour. Much thought goes into children's television and radio programmes; children's books are a flourishing industry, and the education system is respected throughout the world.

Previous page: *A vision of the Netherlands: flat, geometrically laid-out fields, under an immense sky outlining a curtain of trees and a cluster of houses grouped around a church.*

The Romans dug the first canals and some of these still exist. Amsterdam's canal system has protected it from the worst of modern urbanisation, and the elegant old houses continue to gaze upon their pretty distortions in the water.

A Country Reclaimed from the Sea

If the Dutch have finally managed to turn back the sea, control the rivers and halt land erosion, it has been at incalculable cost and in the face of constant setbacks. More often than not, they have had to take two steps back for every step forward. In the 700 years to the beginning of this century they had reclaimed 2007 square miles from the sea and lakes, but over the same period had lost 2186 square miles. Whenever they seemed secure, a high wind and tide would combine to send seas crashing through their flimsy barricades.

The problem is that the Netherlands is not so much flat as saucer-shaped. The bowl of the saucer is several feet below sea level, and if the water rises by only a few inches at certain places, this can mean catastrophe. The flood of the Feast of St Elisabeth, November 18, 1421, was one such disaster. On the previous day an exceptional gale had churned up the waves: the dikes were breached, and the sea surged up the delta of the Rhine, drowning all before it. A hundred thousand people perished, swept away with their animals and their homes, until the waters finally halted below the walls of Dordrecht. The following year the seas surged again, and some of the repairs gave way. The water poured through the gaps and created an inland sea of 166 square miles, strewn with islands where the bullrushes grew so thickly that it was called the Biesbosch (Bullrush Wood); it still exists, though much of it has been restored to dry land through modern drainage methods. The storm in 1570, which 'drove the water to heights never before seen', hit hardest in the north, where many houses on clay foundations broke loose and floated away, sometimes with sleeping families inside unaware of their fate. Tens of thousands of people died, while 94 pigs are still remembered for the manner in which they sailed to safety aboard a floating island of dung.

Cycling knows no limits of age or class in the Netherlands. The Queen, her ministers, peasants, housewives and children all cycle for pleasure, or to go to work or school. There are 12 million bicycles for a population of 14.6 million, and the country is criss-crossed by a network of cycle paths.

So it has continued into modern times. On the night of February 1, 1953, a tremendous storm hit the coast as a spring flood tide was rising. The gale drove the surging waters over dikes, which were undermined and eventually collapsed to let the sea wash across almost all of the southern province of Zeeland, and other areas besides, drowning 1850 people and leaving 70,000 homeless; the cattle stock was almost wiped out. Within hours the inundated region returned to the salt marsh that it had been centuries before; much of Rotterdam was flooded, and in Our Lady's Church of Dordrecht the water lapped beneath the stained glass window depicting the flood of 500 years before. But the indomitable Dutch had learned how to counter-attack, and within four months had put the sea back in its place; by July, the flooded area had been reclaimed.

Dutch rivers are hardly less of a threat than the sea. The Rhine, the Maas (Meuse) and the Scheldt reach the coast in the south, and before man's intervention the Rhine in particular would flood large areas in spring, whenever the run-off from Alpine snows was heavy. Maps from the great age of Dutch navigation in the 16th and 17th centuries show that the rivers were constantly reshaping the land areas, which were broken up by many lakes. The name of Amsterdam's airport, Schipol, means 'the well of ships', which is what it is. The airport is built on the old bed of the Haarlemmermeer, a treacherous stretch of water when the wind whipped up, and the graveyard of many ships. In those days, in farms around the lake, children would dive under the bedclothes during a storm, terrified by the howling of the 'water wolf' outside. Often Haarlemmermeer's waters lapped against the walls of Amsterdam, and washed down the streets of Leyden. When he was made King of the Netherlands, Louis Bonaparte, Napoleon's brother, was so startled by the river floods of 1809 that he wanted to abandon the struggle and dismantle the dikes: he advised that houses should be built on mounds, as they had been long before.

Drying out the sea

'No one knows if this country belongs to the sea or the land,' wrote the 1st-century Roman historian Pliny the Elder. 'An unfortunate race lives there, perched on hills, or rather on low mounds which they have erected with their own hands.' In the centuries that followed, the mounds, known as *terpen*, were linked by dikes, and then, gradually, ways were devised to drain and reclaim land rich in loam carried down by the rivers. Such land became known as polder, from an old word 'pol', meaning a stake, since stakes driven into the water and packed around with seaweed, reeds or any handy rubble, were the basis of the early dikes. The Czech writer Karel Capek neatly summed up the Dutch solution: 'Take a piece of sea, surround it with a wall, then pump it

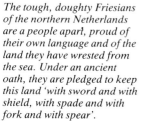

The tough, doughty Friesians of the northern Netherlands are a people apart, proud of their own language and of the land they have wrested from the sea. Under an ancient oath, they are pledged to keep this land 'with sword and with shield, with spade and with fork and with spear'.

dry. . . . Plant grass, let cows eat the grass, milk the cows and make cheese. Send to England.'

Though sluices to discharge trapped ground water and rain water were probably in use a thousand years ago, the big breakthough came with the windmill, in particular the rotating turret version developed in the 16th century. It could operate whatever the wind direction, and pump and keep large areas of reclaimed land thoroughly dry. In the 19th century, steam supplanted wind; three steam engines were able to do the job of hundreds of windmills and drain the Haarlemmermeer, which over the course of four centuries had doubled in size.

This led to grander dreams. Why not drain the Zuiderzee, the immense intrusion of seawater in the north? What had been lake and peat bog in Roman times had by the year 1300 become a hugely swollen bay of the sea eating into the heart of the country. The first plan for draining the Zuiderzee was drawn up by an engineer named Hendrik Stevin in 1667, but the idea was not advanced again for 200 years, and work did not get under way until after the First World War. Various proposals were discussed, including the creation of a single polder of a thousand square miles, but the one decided upon was the concept of Dr Cornelis Lely, a man with a mind worthy of the science fiction of Jules Verne. A dike almost 20 miles long was to contain the Zuiderzee at its mouth, and to turn it into a freshwater lake fed by the River IJssel. This was accomplished by 1932. Then, like pieces dropped into a gigantic jigsaw puzzle, five polders were to be created, one by one, to cover a total of 770 square miles and so provide the Netherlands with another province. The first polder was completed in 1942, and is fully developed. Others were pumped dry in 1957 and 1968 and are under cultivation. A start has been made on a fourth, the big Markerwaard Polder in the south-east sector of the IJsselmeer nearest Amsterdam. But as resistance from environmentalists has stiffened in recent years, its completion has become very unlikely.

The Delta Plan, put into action after the terrible floods of 1953, is a still bolder concept. It involves streamlining and containing the entire southern coast behind an indestructible barrier. Twenty miles of new, very strong North Sea dikes, together with some smaller secondary ones were designed to chop off at their necks the deep arms of the sea, up which the tidal races thrust far inland, and to link together the islands and peninsulas of the delta lands of the Rhine, Maas and Scheldt. Sophisticated techniques were used, and the elimination of hundreds of miles of dangerous coastline is fulfilling all hopes. As well as providing a shield, the delta works with their huge sluices have been termed the stopcock of the Netherlands. They create a number of large freshwater lakes behind the barrier dikes, where before there was salty estuary. Where the country was paradoxically short of fresh water, now it has the benefit of huge reservoirs which can double as leisure resorts. Most of the new dikes carry highways, providing much shortened, vastly swifter coastal routes and the scale of the engineering has to be seen

to be believed. By the time that present plans are completed the indented Dutch coastline will have been reduced in length by about a thousand miles, mostly in the delta region.

During the 17th century, soon after the start of the crusade to wrest land from the sea, the Netherlands was gripped by a strange craze – Tulipomania. The two enterprises of land reclamation and bulb-growing have progressed together ever since, although tulips have never again reached the astronomical prices they fetched in the 1630s. At the height of the tulip frenzy a single bulb changed hands for 4600 florins (plus a fine new carriage and a pair of horses). Tulips had reached the Netherlands from Turkey early in the 17th century and cultivation started in the sandy soil near Haarlem. They quickly spread southwards towards Leyden to form De Bloembollenstreek, to this day the most famous bulbfields in the world. There was also a northern expansion, and today fields of tulips, gladioli, hyacinths, crocuses, daffodils

The many canals of the Netherlands are busy arteries. Small suspension bridges are continually being raised and lowered to allow the boats to pass, while the children wave to the crews.

and narcissi sprout on polder land reclaimed from the Zuiderzee in the north, and on the delta lands in the south.

As well as being one of the country's great industries, flowers and plants are an essential part of Dutch life. They fill the windows of homes and offices, line the streets and brighten the shops, and are cause for shows, parades and pageants. The traffic jams around De Bloembollenstreek in April and May are almost as impressive as the spectacle that is responsible for them.

The fascinating play of light on so much shimmering water is thought by some to account for that other great Dutch product – artists – and the surge of self-confident activity that marked the Golden Age (as the 17th century is called) undoubtedly accounted for

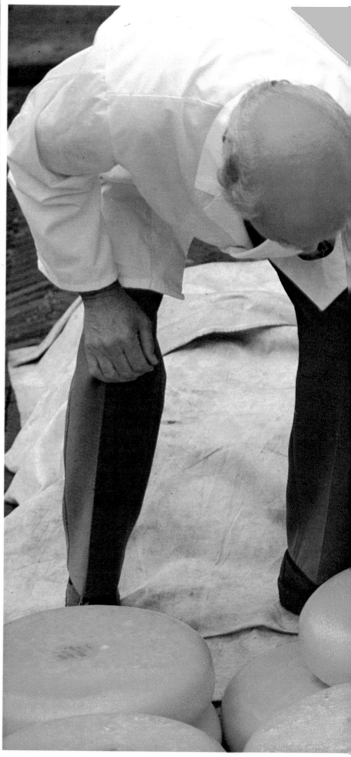

The Dutch cattle industry has made great technological advances since the Second World War, but deals are still made the old way, sealed with a vigorous and loud series of claps as buyer's hand slaps against seller's.

The 'queen of the dikes' – a Friesian cow. The Friesian, with an average production of well over 1000 gallons of milk a year, is the backbone of a dairy industry whose products have been exported for centuries.

Cheese is so associated with the Netherlands that the Dutch are sometimes called kaaskoppen *– cheeseheads. The cheese markets of Gouda, Edam and Alkmaar have kept all their picturesque qualities and attract huge crowds. Daily meals in the Netherlands include thin slices of cheese, eaten with bread and butter.*

the flowering of brilliant artists known as the Dutch Masters. The greatest of these was surely Rembrandt van Rijn (1606–69), a miller's son from Leyden, whose use of light and shadow, and ability to turn a portrait into a metaphysical experience, has been an inspiration to artists ever since.

Once the Golden Age was over the Dutch were rarely without a string of worthy but dull painters to record the fields and cities of their country. Only when Vincent van Gogh erupted into the art world in the 1880s did the Netherlands produce a painter whose stunning use of light and colour could bear comparison with his illustrious forebears.

The urban horseshoe

In the old days only the church spires broke the monotony of the Dutch skyline, and the sound of their carillons mingled pleasingly in the still, clear air. Now the spires have all but disappeared under a tide of construction, rising so fast that a scene can be unrecognisably transformed from one visit to the next. In the Low Countries, a clump of houses or a high-rise building make up a landscape much as the curve of a hill or a valley would elsewhere.

When at the end of the 16th century, after a fierce struggle against the Spanish, the nation gained its independence, this was the most densely populated country in Europe. It was also highly urbanised for its time: during the Golden Age, more than half the

Staircases as steep as ladders make it impossible to carry heavy luggage or large objects to the upper floors of Amsterdam's old houses, so an outside pulley mounted on the roof gable does the job.

In the old days the ports of the Zuiderzee, Zeeland and Friesland were filled with fishing boats that roved as far as the Arctic, and a merchant fleet that brought wood from the Baltic and spices from the Indies. Now pleasure craft have taken over the moorings.

population lived in towns of red-brick houses, usually grouped around a church on the banks of a canal. During the second half of the 19th century, new industries caused some towns to expand greatly, but it was not until after the Second World War that major development throughout the coastal zone led to the phenomenon of the Randstad (Ring Town), a great conurbation bent in the form of a horseshoe to link Utrecht and Amsterdam in the north, with Haarlem, Leyden, The Hague, Delft, Rotterdam and Dordrecht in a wheeling curve to the south and south-east.

The Randstad is no ugly urban sprawl, but rather a chain of highly individual units, linked around so much open country that the green belt concept gets turned inside out, and while it has a pulse which beats to much the same rhythm as a big metropolis like London, it still enjoys an intimate relationship with the countryside. About 40 per cent of the Dutch population live here. No land is wasted; its use is carefully organised and subject to stringent control, with the needs of industry, housing, agriculture and leisure carefully balanced. The Hague is the elegant administrative centre of the country. Amsterdam is the commercial, financial and cultural capital. Rotterdam is the port, and with Leyden, Delft and

Utrecht, these cities are home to universities, superb museums, symphony orchestras and the major media. As in the Golden Age, the maritime region continues to set economic, artistic and intellectual standards for the rest of the country.

More than canals and windmills

Amsterdam and Rotterdam have always been great rivals. While Amsterdam remains the first city of the Netherlands, Rotterdam has risen from the ashes of war to create in Europoort the biggest and busiest harbour in the world. The task was facilitated by Nazi bombers, which obliterated its tangled old core by razing 30,000 buildings in the course of a few hours on May 14, 1940. The new city is no Old Dutch Master, but an extremely efficient machine of concrete, steel and glass.

Amsterdam, by contrast, has the greatest number of listed buildings for any city in Europe: more than 7000 structures under official care, ranging from Rembrandt's home to the house where for two years

Anne Frank hid and wrote her immensely moving diary, until she was discovered and deported to the Auschwitz death camp. Amsterdam (it means Dam on the River Amstel) retains the atmosphere of the early 17th century, when it was in its prime as a trading port. Still lining its canals are houses whose upper storeys were once filled with tea, spices, silks and furs, and its patrician mansions seem haunted by the spirits of their former owners, the proud 'burghers' who sat for Rembrandt and Frans Hals. The concentric rings of canals are Amsterdam's marvel: in precise, symmetrical order they cut a

These beautiful houses, so closely packed together, date back to the heroic days when the people of the Low Countries freed themselves from Spanish rule and founded a merchant republic which soon became one of the richest nations in Europe.

series of crescents, like so many defensive moats, which is what some of them originally were.

Urban life is not confined to the Randstad loop. There is Groningen, under the tower belfry of St Martin's, which strikes the hours so slowly that it seems permanently behind the times; there is Arnhem on the Rhine, poignant with its memories of gallant tragedy in 1944; Haarlem, home of the tulip and Frans Hals; Gouda, producer of cheese; Nijmegen, standing high above the Waal since Roman times; quaint Maastricht, which has withstood 21 sieges,

including one in which the musketeer D'Artagnan gave his life to save the Duke of Marlborough, Winston Churchill's most celebrated ancestor; equally battered Breda, where Charles II lived in exile during Cromwell's rule; 's Hertogenbosch (usually abbreviated to Den Bosch), famous for its Gothic cathedral; there is hardly a town in the Netherlands that is not soaked in history.

The popular picture of rural Holland is of flat polders, canals and windmills. It is justified, in as much as more than half the country is reclaimed, or at least dike-protected land, and just enough wind-mills have survived (around 900 out of a one-time 16,000) to complete the picture. This is the scene of much of the western half of the country, where the flat acres of cultivation are broken only by waterways in which craft cruise between fields that stretch away to some distant confluence with the sky.

But the Netherlands is much more than this.

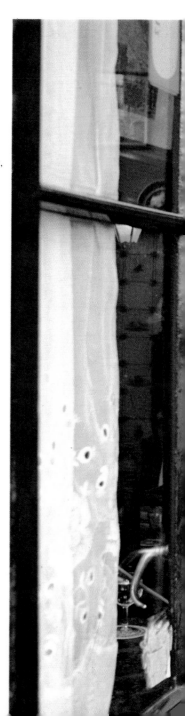

Since its discovery by the world's hippies in the 1960s, the square known as the Dam, opposite the huge Royal Palace, has become the meeting point for tourists in Amsterdam. It lies in the old part of town, near the rosse buurt *or red-light district.*

Zeeland is a province of fertile islands and peninsulas divided by wide channels that are now contained by the Delta Plan, while Limburg in the south-east has pretty wooded hills and valleys, including the country's highest peak (at just over 1000 feet!). South to north, the central and eastern Netherlands is a belt of heath and woodland. Some of it is quiet and remote, as the name of part of this area – Achterhoek (Back Corner) – indicates. North again, the provinces of Drenthe and Groningen have an ancient history hidden in burial mounds and peat workings, and the shape of many villages reveal their origins as man-made hillocks: the *terpen*, which were the first stage in land reclamation thousands of years ago. Through much of the central and eastern region the landscape is varied and softened by low hills, and beech and aspen woods are interspersed with sandy plains carpeted with heather. Then come the wide waterways of southern Friesland, from whose banks can be seen the breezy and popular resorts of the Friesian Islands, which mark the shoreline as it was 2000 years ago.

To drive by night, from the hilly country down into the bowl, is to gain a magical sense of the Dutch experience. The landscape becomes so flat that it is indistinguishable from the sky; then come the irregular outlines of the towns, following each other with increasing rapidity. As the Dutch prefer not to draw their curtains, after dark the canals glitter with starry reflections. A single glance can take in everything that moves over the night plain: crowded motorways criss-cross in every direction, merging and separating with coiling curves of light like glowing serpents; electric trains dash at top speed across darkened fields also traversed by snail-like lighters and barges; on top of a dike a solitary cyclist stands, a tiny silhouette under the immense dome of sky.

The Dutch word gezelligheid *means the moments spent relaxing with family or friends over a cup of coffee or a glass of beer.*

The pigeonhole mentality

The 12 provinces have always enjoyed a measure of autonomy, and have kept their distinctive personalities. If there is a great contrast in landscape for such a small country, this is also true of the attitudes of the people; on the one hand Friesland, introvert and reserved, and on the other Limburg, extrovert and relaxed; the austerity of the Groningen people contrasts with the easy-going approach of Brabanters. Again, there is a world of difference between the shipowners and dockers of Rotterdam and the civil servants of The Hague, only 12 miles away. In Zeeland, on the dangerous southern coast, and in Friesland and Groningen in the north, the constant fight against the elements has fostered a disciplined spirit that constrasts with the more relaxed attitudes in the higher and drier 'old land' of the interior. As well as this west-east divide, the Rhine and Maas flow side by side to divide the country between the Protestant north and the Catholic south. Down in Brabant and Limburg, the people speak in melodious singing tones that find plenty of expression during the pre-Lent carnivals. There are those in the north who regard Limburg almost as a mistake, an alien intrusion; its capital Maastrict, astride the Maas, is almost completely surrounded by Belgium.

A spirit of stubborn defiance was instilled from early times. Julius Caesar's Romans were fiercely resisted, and they never completely subdued the Friesians. In the Middle Ages, as commerce prospered, town leaders began to treat their overlords as equals, and freedom, once established, could never be suppressed. It was his inability to understand this that led to the defeat of Philip II of Spain. In 1581 seven provinces declared their independence, but even at the height of this struggle against oppression some provinces and cities refused to join in the uprising, for there is a tendency among the Dutch to resist being forced into line, whatever the cause; it is in this respect that they differ most from their German neighbours.

All of this experience, the centuries of struggle against nature and against foreign domination, and of crowded confinement in the few dry regions, has gone into the making of the Dutch character, which contrives to combine a strong individualism with a respect for order and sense of community. As individualists the Dutch maintain a tradition of liberal toleration, and are first among Europeans in their defence of human rights. In crowded conditions

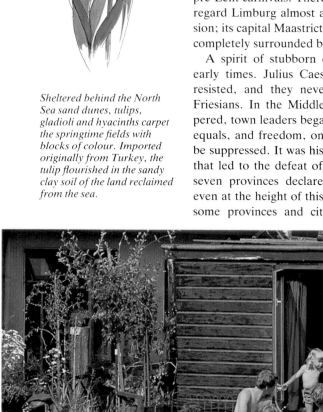

Sheltered behind the North Sea sand dunes, tulips, gladioli and hyacinths carpet the springtime fields with blocks of colour. Imported originally from Turkey, the tulip flourished in the sandy clay soil of the land reclaimed from the sea.

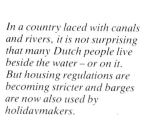

The small wooden houses around Zaan are reminders of the 17th century, when this was the region of Europe's finest shipyards. With few trees, the Dutch had to import their timber from the Baltic. Windmills then drove the saws which turned the logs into ships' planks. The Tsar Peter the Great worked as a shipwright here in 1697, before going on to Deptford on the Thames, and then returning home to create a Russian fleet.

In a country laced with canals and rivers, it is not surprising that many Dutch people live beside the water – or on it. But housing regulations are becoming stricter and barges are now also used by holidaymakers.

tolerance is an important asset, but it has to go alongside an attention to tidiness and order. The Dutch personality is a successful combination of these requirements.

To understand the Netherlands fully, the depth of religious and ideological divisions needs to be appreciated. Limburg and Brabant in the south are mainly Catholic, and their approach to life is quite different from that of the Protestantism of Zeeland and the provinces 'north of the rivers'. Where Catholic and Protestant live side by side some segregation is still the rule, despite some relaxation in recent years. This has led to a unique social system of parallel communities. This is known as the *zuilen*, from a word meaning pillars. From the cradle to the grave most Dutch people used to – and to some extent still do – live within their *zuil*, the religious or ideological group into which each has been born. If the family is Catholic, the baby will be born in a Catholic clinic, go to Catholic schools and graduate from a Catholic university. There are still Catholic radio and television stations, a Catholic press, Catholic political parties and trade unions: an entire infrastructure set apart from those of other Dutch communities.

To witness the zuilen in full flower, look to the

media: there are Protestant, Catholic, socialist and liberal television channels, each headed by a board of directors with complete control over programmes. The zuilen encourage what the Dutch call the 'pigeonhole spirit' (*hokjesgeest*), with everyone living in their own compartment, with their own standards, convictions and prejudices. Yet they also create opportunities for stimulating debate, for the system only works if every zuil is free to express its opinions. This means that the media abounds in diametrically opposed viewpoints; so much so that until 1956 it was considered a sin for Catholics to listen to Protestant radio. However, since the 1960s the Netherlands has been subject to a process of secularisation which seems to have undermined the traditional zuilen mentality.

The result of such narrowness was a certain tension in the Dutch people. In the Netherlands, everyone has a right to his or her own opinions, so long as they do not interfere with those of their neighbours. Emotions need to be kept under tight control, and here the Dutch rely upon *nuchterheid*, a word with no English equivalent. It implies a need to be reasonable and objective at all times; never to be influenced by first impressions or get carried away, and always to think things over carefully and to weigh up each word. Such caution becomes second nature, and sometimes makes decision-taking a laborious process. In business dealings with the Dutch, or in politics, the delays, and the impression of sometimes proceeding backwards, can put a severe strain on negotiations. Yet the achievements of the Netherlands and its people are evidence that they get there in the end.

Netjes means to be clean and tidy, and Dutch women are extremely so. Whenever the sun shines, the family's washing waves joyfully in the wind that blows freely across this flat land.

Foreign visitors have for centuries been struck by the amount of time that Dutch housewives spend in cleaning, scrubbing and polishing – they take great pride in their homes.

Urbanised since the Middle Ages, the Netherlands have many fine examples of the neat and distinctive Dutch domestic architecture, old and new. Traditional materials such as brick are still used.

Keeping the home fire burning

Almost fifteen million people crowd into this little kingdom of 13,000 square miles: more than a thousand to every square mile. Space is at a premium – so having conquered the sea, the Dutch have launched themselves into the air with the construction of high-rise blocks with the regimented architecture of a crossword. It is hardly the ideal environment for clogs and the tulip patch, but traditional Dutch ways of life are not allowed to die, however much circumstances change. Every morning about four million Dutch people go to work; despite the growing number of women who work, nearly

The first Dutch adventurers were the fishermen. For unknown reasons catches of herring in the Baltic Sea declined in the 14th century, forcing fishermen to try their luck in the North Sea, around Spitzbergen and other stormy regions. This experience encouraged the merchant adventurers who, from the 16th century, set up markets all round the world.

three million still stay at home and maintain the tradition of neat, spotless households. As in the 'good old days', whether in modern block, little brick house or on the farm, they wash, scrub, polish, dust and sweep, and then water the colourful plants that fill the window-sills and living rooms.

The Dutch are home lovers: so much so that their personalities seem to change the moment they cross the threshold. At home they are relaxed, serene and confident, while in public they sometimes appear awkward and reticent. The contrast is striking enough to amount to a national split personality. Unlike the immigrants from their former colonies in the East Indies, or southern Europeans, to whom the street is a second home, the Dutch never seem to be completely relaxed in public; watch them dance, and see how many look as though they are still wearing clogs. Part of it is shyness, compounded by the introversion forced upon society by the limitations of zuilen, and so social interplay involves a subtlety that foreigners need to understand if they wish to become a part of it; in particular, they need to appreciate the *gezelligheid*, another untranslatable expression, which implies a welcome to the home but which governs relations in the office, factory and just about anywhere else. *Gezelligheid* can be established over a cup of tea or coffee, or a drink.

Birthdays and anniveraries are very important. A special calendar hangs in every home, marked with the birthdays of family, friends, neighbours and

The little port of Marken was once a busy fishing town, but now its main business is tourism. The interiors of the homes are as compact and tidy as ships' cabins.

The Dutch quickly realised that salt preserved herring, and by the Middle Ages were exporting their catch to all corners of Europe. In spring everyone in the Netherlands enjoys fresh fillets of raw fish, sometimes accompanied by raw onion.

colleagues. To forget any is a serious matter, and quite unforgivable in the case of a close relation. Some anniversaries are especially significant. The 50th, referred to as 'Meeting Abraham', is an occasion for a party that lasts all night. To 'meet Abraham' is a great moment in the life of a person or an enterprise, and calls for heavy consumption of beer and ice-cold Dutch gin. Success in a school exam is another cause for celebration, and the school bag will be hung from a window, along with the national flag, just to let the world know.

The Dutch St Nicholas season begins earlier than the British Christmas, in late October, when fancifully shaped marzipan and spicy cakes and biscuits appear in the shops. This is followed on November 21, by the arrival of the saint himself – Sinterklaas, as the Dutch call him. He has the same white beard and red robe as his English-speaking counterpart, but he has come from Spain instead of the North Pole; he carries a bishop's golden crook, and is attended by a Moorish servant, Zwarte Piet, or Black Peter. All of Amsterdam turns out to welcome him, and at that moment Sinterklazen suddenly make their appearance throughout the country.

St Nicholas's Day, December 6, is marked by families in a manner unchanged since the 17th century, as depicted by some of the masters of the Dutch school. Parents and children receive elaborately wrapped presents; these are opened to applause and much laughter, for a poem accompanies each gift. For weeks everyone has been concocting rhymes, with stifled laughter announcing each particularly pleasing invention, for the rhyme mocks some foible of the recipient, who is obliged to read it aloud. A collection of these verses would reveal more about the joys, sorrows, fears and motivations of the Dutch people than any academic analysis.

Christmas itself was not a big family occasion until recently, but under Anglo-American influence, and to the delight of the shops, the St Nicholas festivities have been extended to incorporate December 25, and most Dutch families have a Christmas tree and exchange cards. New Year's Eve is another celebratory occasion adopted from abroad, but the Dutch hardly lack traditional celebrations of their own. Frolicking on frozen canals has been associated with this country since the 17th-century painters popularized the concept, and ice-skating races are still a

Delftware dates back to the 17th century, and was inspired by porcelain imported from China. The best potters were soon centred in the delightful town of Delft, which produces the famous Delft blue.

focus of fun, with much feasting and drinking afterwards. The most famous is the Elfstedentocht, the Eleven Towns race held in Friesland. It starts at 7 o'clock in the morning, and covers a 125-mile course around 11 towns; some competitors are still doggedly skating at midnight. Obviously, the race can only be held in those years when the weather is cold enough to freeze the canals.

The Dutch enjoy their food, and tend to be as generous with the portions as they are with the butter that goes into their recipes, which can be a challenge to the digestion of visitors. Favourites include *erwtensoep* (a thick pea soup with sausage or bacon), *uitsmijters* (buttered bread topped with ham or cheese, two or three fried eggs and pickles) and *pannekoeken* (big pancakes in a thick brown syrup called *stroop*, and a topping that can range from banana to bacon). Indonesian food from the colonial past has also become part of the national fare, and includes *bami* (pork, vegetables and noodles mixed with spices) and *rijstaffel* (savouries served with rice and chutney).

Regal simplicity

For centuries, the fortunes of the Netherlands have been inextricably bound up with those of the House of Orange-Nassau, which also briefly ruled Britain when the Protestant William and Mary succeeded the Catholic James II in the Glorious Revolution of 1688.

The House of Orange seems to be as secure as ever: according to an opinion poll taken in 1980, 92 per cent of Dutch people support the monarchy, which has barely been touched by the changes that have affected the Church, family life, the universities, politics and attitudes in general. The marriage in 1966 of the future queen Beatrix to the German commoner Claus von Amsberg, who had been in the Hitler Youth and the Germany Army during the Second World War, sparked some protests. These quickly died down after the birth of their son Willem-

The Netherlands' heavy, damp soil needs solid, warm and watertight footwear. The traditional sabot (wooden clog), kept outside on the doorstep and stuffed with straw for warmth in winter, is still the solution in the country, though it has disappeared from the towns.

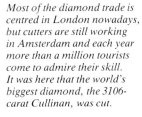

Most of the diamond trade is centred in London nowadays, but cutters are still working in Amsterdam and each year more than a million tourists come to admire their skill. It was here that the world's biggest diamond, the 3106-carat Cullinan, was cut.

Crisp, spiced ginger biscuits made in fancifully shaped moulds are a feature of St Nicholas' Day (December 6), an important holiday in the Netherlands. So is taai-taai (spiced cake) in the form of animals, and banketleller, an almond-filled pastry in the shape of an initial. This St Nicholas, also called Sinterklaas, not only arrives well ahead of his non-Dutch twin, but comes from Spain, not the North Pole.

Alexander in 1967. He is the first male in the House of Orange since William III died in 1890. When an opinion poll was held to determine a popular favourite for president (just supposing the country should decide to become a republic), the overwhelming vote was for the Queen. The Queen's birthday, which by tradition is celebrated on April 30, is an important national holiday, when the cities are bedecked with royal standards and orange decorations. This is also the occasion when thousands of people file past the steps of the royal palace, on which the Queen and her family stand to receive gifts of flowers. The royal opening of parliament on the third Tuesday in September is a further opportunity for displays of loyalty.

Even if the coach she uses on this occasion is

Centuries before environmentalists advocated wind power as a clean energy source, the windmill was draining the water meadows and powering the Netherlands. Most windmills were replaced by steam-driven pumps in the 19th century, but the 900 that remain are lovingly preserved.

golden, the Queen's demeanour is very relaxed. Simplicity has long been a watchword with Dutch royalty, as the sober mien of their portraits demonstrates. William the Silent, dubbed 'Father of his Country' for leading the revolt against Spain, had lived at the Spanish court of Charles V, but he took away none of its extravagant ways. His clothing, according to an English visitor, was 'such as a clerk of low birth from one of our country inns would have been ashamed to wear in town.'

Three hundred years later Queen Wilhelmina avoided all display of wealth and became a kind of Dutch Queen Victoria to her loyal subjects. She was greatly admired for the stubbornness and sense of duty that she displayed during her wartime exile in London. Her daughter Juliana, mother of the present queen, was not so stiff, and her unaffected behaviour brought her closer to the average citizen, who saw in her their own best qualities. As 'unifier, temporiser, an example to all', the role of the monarch is to strike a 'just mean between the selfishness of the Liberals, the self-righteousness of the Christians, and the resentment of the Socialists, who are none of them havens of democratic tolerance', according to one Dutch journalist.

So what are these national qualities that the Dutch crown seeks to enshrine? She is outstandingly hardworking and thrifty, with an excellent business sense and great tolerance, according to the opinion of other Europeans as collected for a 1973 survey. When they themselves were questioned, the Dutch completely agreed with this point of view.

In winter the Dutch skate along the canals, sometimes alone, sometimes in family groups, stopping occasionally at a stall to enjoy a bowl of erwtensoep – *hot, thick split-pea soup.*

Germany

From rags to riches in one generation, the German
economic miracle is a story to cheer the sternest banker's heart.
After the darkest night in the nation's history, the country that gave
Europe Beethoven, Goethe and the fairy stories of the Brothers Grimm is
again the epitome of order and a bulwark of stability. From the depths
of the Black Forest to the steel and glass pinnacle of a Berlin
office block, Germany is building a future on the foundations
of the best traditions of its past.

Rüdesheim is the gateway to 'Romantic Germany', the start of the steep Bingen Gap, where the slopes of the foothills are striped with vineyards. While waiting for their Rhine cruise boat, tourists prowl the wine bars of the narrow Drosselgasse, or inspect the 12th-century Bromserburg, one of the oldest of all the Rhine castles.

Previous page: *Germans drink a lot of beer, about 35 gallons a year, and a lot of beers – there are 1300 breweries. What all Germans expect to get when they order 'ein Bier' is* Vollbier, *which has a maximum 4 per cent alcohol, whereas 'ein Bock', or* Bockbier, *can be 5.5 per cent proof.*

A Land of Legend and Success

The view that the visitor retains of modern Germany depends on the purpose of his journey – business or pleasure. Many tourists imagine that the whole of Germany is like an enchantingly beautiful Bavaria and forget the car plants, the chemical works and the steel mills. Moreover, they rarely think to see the rest of the country: the indented North Sea coastline, with its snug fishing ports and open dunes; the wide Baltic beaches where in summer the water is almost as warm as the Mediterranean; the gently rolling central plain that rises towards the wooded slopes of the Alps; or the soaring southern peaks with their magnificent scenery and their thriving winter sports centres to match.

Just as it is unrealistic to expect all of Germany to look like Bavaria, so the alternative vision of the businessman can be equally false. There certainly are huge cities with stark, tall buildings, but post-war reconstruction has been executed with taste, and many old districts destroyed in the Second World War have been skilfully restored. Many others escaped wartime devastation and remain just as they were down the centuries. Peaceful university towns like Marburg in the centre of the country and Tübingen in the south-west are reminders that Germany is a land of philosophers, musicians and poets, in which even a modest town has its theatre and opera house. On a visit to Frankfurt or Wetzlar in central Germany little effort is required to imagine the presence of Goethe, or to catch echoes of a Schümann piano concerto along the tree-shaded banks of the Rhine. The fanciful castles built by Ludwig II of Bavaria are full of Wagnerian memories, and along the little country roads of Swabia Schubert's Wanderer still seems to lament his hopeless love. Despite its modern prosperity, Germany is still a fairy-tale country, the land of tall Gothic spires, richly decorated town halls and churches and half-timbered houses.

To get to the roots of it all, go to Trier in the west of the country close to the border with Luxembourg, Germany's oldest town, where even the quality of the light seems to be striking and different: pure as crystal in the morning, golden bright at noon, and softly caressing at dusk, which is a very good time to arrive. The Emperor Augustus is credited with founding Trier in 15 BC, but the area was settled by a tribe called the Treveri long before that – so long that local tradition makes it 1300 years older than Rome itself. The Romans made Trier their northern capital, and built so mightily that today it boasts some of the biggest and best chunks of Roman remains anywhere. The 2nd-century Porta Nigra, the mightiest gateway in the entire Roman Empire, still dominates the city, while the Aula Palatina, a basilica built by the Emperor Constantine, is a triumph of Roman design to be compared only with the Pantheon in Rome. It has survived to serve now as a

Freiburg, near the Black Forest, is a joyful university town with many pubs and open-air restaurants. Five centuries of Austrian rule may have contributed to its delightful atmosphere. Around its gothic Minster of Our Lady is one of Germany's most picturesque and bustling markets.

The Elbe widens to form the huge harbour of Hamburg while still more than 70 miles from the North Sea. The port has many docks able to take ocean-going ships and its 6-square-mile Speicherstadt (warehouse town) is the biggest storage complex in the world. Hamburg is also a major commercial and industrial centre. There are more millionaires here than anywhere else in Germany.

Protestant parish church. There are Roman baths, a Roman amphitheatre and a Roman bridge. Even the medieval cathedral rests on Roman foundations. A few steps from the cathedral is the Hauptmarkt, one of the most picturesque of all German market-places and a marvellously instructive jumble of architectural history.

German towns did not usually grow up in the shadow of a church or cathedral, as in so many other countries, but around the town hall, the *Rathaus*. The country was only united under the Prussian chancellor Bismarck's leadership in 1871; before that, towns were frequently the capitals of small independent states, or independent in their own right. The square in front of the town hall was the marketplace, and the gathering point in times of decision and crisis. Today, the main business areas and most fashionable shopping centres are grouped around these squares, which provide plenty of room to move around. Below every *Rathaus* are spacious cellars, cool in summer, warm in winter, the lair of good restaurants that stay open late at night. A short

Many large towns have grown on the banks of the rivers and canals of Germany. The barges and cargo vessels that crowd these waterways provide an efficient means of transporting goods to and from industrial centres.

walk away will be the cathedral, its style varying from pure Romanesque, as in Worms and Speyer, to the Gothic extravagances of Cologne and Lübeck, with the most elaborate spires in Christendom. So it is with Trier. The town band and the organ-grinder with his monkey still exercise in the square where Roman emperors and Charlemagne once trod, and where early last century a youthful Karl Marx came and did his shopping.

Mosel wine and Rhinegold

The old villages with their half-timbered houses and tiled roofs cluster along the banks of the Mosel, between vineyards with vines trained along high trellises. This used to be the classic destination of those in search of romantic Germany, and of 'the feeling of relish and well-being' reported by Goethe on a boat trip from Trier to Koblenz in 1792. The poet did not have to contend with the pollution that on occasion has filled the river with dead fish, and put paid to the famous *Moselhecht* (fresh pike). Another difference since his time is that European Community economics have forced some growers of the fruity white wines that he so much admired out of business; but the romance of the region continues to work its spell. People from Koblenz come at weekends to drink the wine, picnic and walk in the forests, and in the evenings, hikers and cyclists gather around long

The St Pauli wharves are the departure point for cruises on the Elbe, or around Hamburg's great harbour. Nearby is St Pauli, notorious for its daring nightlife.

German cars have conquered the world, with Mercedes, Porsche, BMW and Volkswagen among the leading manufacturers. There is a fine motor museum in the main Daimler-Benz factory in Stuttgart, which celebrates all the Mercedes racing triumphs.

tables set out on the terraces of the beautiful castles that loom over each lazy bend of the river.

Those who venture into the deep woods may chance upon Eltz, a castle worthy of Sleeping Beauty. To reach this enchanting clutter of towers and crenellations that has been in the same family for more than 800 years, you climb a rough track through a fairy-tale forest, full of rippling water and birdsong, and brushwood shaken occasionally by a startled rabbit or a squirrel.

The Mosel winds through the country south of the

Sausages come in tremendous variety. Grilled or boiled, and served in a bun, they provide a quick meal for people in a hurry. Other varieties stand on ceremony: for instance, Weisswürstel, the small white sausages of Munich, should only be served in the morning. Connoisseurs say that they must 'never hear the clock strike twelve'.

Pils is a lager with a slightly bitter taste and a sparkling colour. It is a Dortmund speciality. Dunkles Bier, darker, heavier and sweeter, is made with roasted malt.

Small uniformed figures have been made in the Black Forest villages and sold in Nürnburg since the Middle Ages. There used to be hundreds of wood-carvers in the town, and the wooden-toy industry still thrives there.

Eifel Mountains, a haunt of roebuck and fallow deer, with signposted forest trails that cross the frontiers into Belgium and Luxembourg. The forests shroud villages that look like illustrations from medieval manuscripts, and abbeys and churches that surprise by being quite real. In spring, the hills are covered with golden broom and flowering juniper bushes. In a region where time seems to stand still, a horse-drawn mail coach links several villages, and a special stamp is issued for the letters it carries.

The Mosel reaches the Rhine at Koblenz, an ideal starting point for an exploration of the romantic glories of the river that inspired Mary Shelley and Thomas Carlyle, and countless others since the Romans (they were the first tourists, leaving behind a lead medallion engraved with a view of Mainz and the greeting: 'Happy days from the banks of the Rhine'). Armies have surged up and down the narrow valley of the Middle Rhine in the same substantial numbers as the modern sightseers, and each sharp crag seems to be topped by its melancholy fortress. 'What lives did the ancient inhabitants of

Houses with steeply pitched roofs and distinctive gables line the streets around the Marketplatz and Rathausplatz in Hamburg. The gables can be plain, or elaborately decorated.

these crumbling ruins lead?' the poet Shelley's widow wanted to know as she sailed by, more than a century ago. She had the answer: 'The occupation of the men was war; that of the women to hope, to fear, to pray, and to embroider.'

The great river fascinates with its swift currents and black rocks barely showing above the water, and is full of legends. Lohengrin, who was originally the son of Parsifal, the hero of the quest for the Holy Grail, appeared below the castle of Cleves, while the mythical water nymph Lorelei sang from her steep rock to lure boatmen to their deaths in revenge for her suicide, which was provoked by an unfaithful lover. Here was the cave of Snow White's seven dwarfs, and every German knows the song of the Nibelungs, the 13th-century poem about the terrible fight between the Burgundians and the Huns, and how the treacherous Hagen, beheaded by Kriemhild with the dragon-slayer Siegfried's sword, still kept the secret of where he had hidden the treasure – in the Rhine!

But the Rhine's romantic associations do not diminish its purpose as a working river. If you stop for the night, and sleep in a room overlooking the water, the engines of barge convoys will remind you that this is an international highway of trade.

The eagle, a universal symbol of speed, power, nobility and military strength, featured on the uniforms of Prussian soldiers before becoming the emblem of the German Army. The bird itself is now extremely rare in Germany and throughout Europe and is protected by stringent laws.

Dairy and beef farming dominate German agriculture and meet 85 per cent of domestic needs. Although the amount of land devoted to farming is steadily shrinking, improved methods have kept production levels constant.

Rothenburg is a 16th-century town, with cobbled streets, fountains and wrought-iron signs over the shop doors. Its wall and battlements survive, as does a unique collection of cages, chastity belts and other instruments of correction and punishment.

Witches and goblins

The mother lode of fantasy, the source of so much enchantment, is not along the Rhine, or anywhere else that it might be expected, but in Kassel, an industrial centre in the heart of Germany and the seat of various Federal courts. Kassel was also the source of all those Hessian troops hired to fight for Britain in the American War of Independence. This did not spare it from British bombers in the Second World War, and the city was almost totally destroyed – so much so that a large part of the municipal area is green open space. Yet what survived was sufficient for it to strike out in an exciting new direction. The Fridericianum, Europe's earliest museum building, which was rebuilt after the last war staged the first *Dokumenta* in 1955, a trend-setting exhibition of modern art that has become a regular event and the biggest show of its kind in the world. Every four years, dealers and connnoisseurs, and the artists themselves, take over the city.

In 1986, Kassel had cause for another sort of celebration: the 200th birthday of Wilhelm Grimm who, together with his brother Jacob created the famous book of fairy tales which have been translated into more than 140 languages. The brothers were studying the sources of the German language, and while compiling a linguistic encyclopedia, gathered their collection of chilling legends, frightening folk tales and magical deeds. The Grimms worked together in Kassel for more than 30 years, and it is for this reason that the neighbouring Hesse and Weser countryside features so strongly in the collection, and sticks firmly in the minds of children all over the world.

In the Middle Ages, when many of the fairy tales evolved, Frankfurt was the scene of important regional fairs, mixtures of trade and entertainment. Today it is at the hub of a network of air, road and rail routes that make it the most accessible place in Germany and a favourite venue of modern international trade fairs. Yet even here, medieval remnants survive amid the steel and glass, and the municipal woods are among the largest of any German town.

A few miles from Frankfurt, along the banks of the

O Tannenbaum. . . . One of the best known German songs praises the steadfastness of the evergreen pine tree of Bavaria and the Black Forest, which starred as the decorated centrepiece of German Christmases long before Prince Albert introduced the Christmas tree to Britain in the middle of the 19th century.

River Main, on the old trade route to Leipzig, a monument in the market square of Hanau commemorates the Grimm brothers who were born here. Then comes Gelnhausen, where the Emperor Barbarossa built a castle in the 12th century; from here the road winds through the picturesque Kinzig Valley, past crooked lanes of half-timbered houses to Steinau an der Strasse, where the Grimms spent their childhood in the old (even then) Amytshaus, or municipal office, where their father was employed as a legal official.

This region is known as the Bergwinkel and has associations as romantic as it is beautiful, with a forest eminently suitable for a wicked witch, and a towering castle just right for an enchanted princess. Steinau is the home of Die Holzköppe, a puppet theatre famous for its productions of fairy tales. More memories of the Grimms, and of medieval knights, mingle in Schlüchtern, a few miles along the road which then proceeds to Fulda. In 744 a Benedictine abbey was founded here, and its monks were largely responsible for the spread of Christianity in Germany. It is half-timbered territory all the way from here to Marburg, where the Grimms began their research into folk-tales, and nearby is the Schwalm, best known as Little Red Riding Hood Country. The distinctive costume of the tale is still to be seen hereabouts. The Brothers Grimm Museum is

A wedding or holiday in the Black Forest is a reason for the mountain people to wear their richly adorned traditional costumes. This version from Gutachtal features the Bollenhut, a hat with monster pompoms – red for young girls and black for married women. The white bodice with puffed sleeves is worn with an embroidered collar trimmed with beads. Coloured woollen stockings complete the outfit.

A cuckoo clock keeps time in this tavern with rustic furniture and panelled walls decorated by a local artist. The beer is served in pretty blue patterned china tankards.

in Kassel, which is just to the north, and north again lies Göttingen, where the medieval atmosphere has proved no impediment to advanced thought, for more than 30 Nobel Prize winners have studied or taught at its university. From Göttingen the fairy trail descends the dreamy valley of the Weser, in a 500-year slumber since the glory days of the Holy Roman Empire. The Grimms travelled this way, and among the many stories they collected was that of the Sleeping Beauty, who was kissed awake in the Sababurg, a castle in the Reinhardswald forest.

If most fairy tales spring from folk memory, then some tales from the Weser are based on known fact. Baron von Munchhausen, a spinner of tall tales, was a real 18th-century personality who served as a soldier in Russia and Turkey, and returned with the stories that were to turn him into a legend. The Pied Piper of Hamelin (Hameln) was a man who, in 1284, managed to rid the town of a plague of rats and, when the village elders refused to pay him, took revenge by luring away 130 boys and girls while their parents were in church. Some historians suspect that the kidnapped children were carried off to settlements in the east of the country while others claim that the children were taken to join the Children's Crusade by ardently pious clergymen in the 13th century. If so, the piper danced them through the forests and meadows of the Harz, a mountain range where (so they say) you might still catch a glimpse of a goblin or a witch. On the eve of May 1, Walpurgis Night, the witches are supposed to take off on their broomsticks to rendezvous with the Devil on top of the highest mountains of the Harz range.

The Weser gets down to serious business when it reaches Bremen, the country's second port after Hamburg. It is said that in the year 449 the Saxons set out from here to conquer England. Beyond,

Pollution from industrial centres is an ever present threat to Germany's forests. Some have been turned into National Parks, while others supply the timber industry.

A thatched house near Lüneburg Heath. Big double doors open onto the Diele, *a huge room where, in the past, people and their animals lived together. Traditionally, these houses had no chimneys, and the smoke escaped through cracks in the roof. Wooden horses' heads were sometimes nailed to the gable in order to ward off bad luck.*

between the Baltic and the North Sea, is a wide marshy plain in the west and wooded hills in the east stretching to the Danish peninsula. Sunset is the best time to arrive at the North Sea, especially at a small port like Husum, where the steamers depart for Heligoland in the summer. A soft light fills the sky, while the air is alive with seagulls, plovers and swallows. The small hotels are named after characters in local poetry, the rooms have light-coloured wooden furniture, and you dine on herring, shrimps and black bread. The people here have battled against the sea, just like the Dutch. To absorb the atmosphere fully, walk along the beach when the setting sun is glinting on the water between the dikes, and on the sails of the windmills, and listen out for the melancholy cry of wild geese overhead.

Inland is Lüneburg Heath. In summer, the ground

The Hofbräuhaus is the most famous beer hall in Munich. In its many smoke-filled rooms and shady courtyards the orchestras play popular songs and the drinkers join in the choruses. Vigilant waitresses see that order is maintained.

East of Marburg is Little Red Riding Hood Country: the story originated here and the costume is sometimes still worn. This was one of many local folk stories collected by the Brothers Grimm in the early 19th century.

is carpeted with mauve heather, while conifers, birches and juniper bushes flourish along roads where no car is allowed. The entire 75 square miles is a protected nature reserve, though it is a curious fact that the area is a consequence of the wholesale destruction of nature. Lüneburg is built on salt deposits, and through centuries of exploitation all the trees were cut down to use as fuel in the extraction process. A heath was the result.

Ludwig's theatrical castles

The quickest way south is by autobahn, one of the famous motorways that are just as impressive as you might expect. They have made as much impact on Germany as its poetic past, and film-makers have often used them to illustrate modern restlessness.

South to Bavaria, to high peaks hiding lakes with deserted shores like the Königsee, whose dark waters are lost in the shadows of towering cliffs. The landscape is dotted with richly decorated Baroque

and Rococo abbeys and churches. But to many, Bavaria means the theatrical castles of Ludwig II, whose frenzy for building almost bankrupted his country. Hohenschwangau, a medieval fortress re-built by his father, was his childhood home and gave him the inspiration to build Neuschwanstein, a fantasy of white towers and pinnacles perched on a limestone cliff. This was the eccentric Ludwig's idea of how a knight's castle should look, and at night he would stand on the Marienbrug, the bridge over the deep ravine, and gaze at the lights blazing from every empty window. Linderhof is a Baroque extravaganza, a frozen meringue whose park is filled with waterfalls, fountains and ornamental ponds, a Moorish pavilion and a grotto, with a lake upon which

The Oktoberfest, or October Festival, in Munich. Huge beer tents – Bierzelte – are set up and oxen are roasted on spits in a fairground atmosphere. During the fortnight of the festival the bars will sell more than 3 million litres (5.3 million pints) of beer, brought to the tent bars in horse-drawn carts.

During the Oktoberfest, some Munichers wear their celebrated traditional costume. The leather trousers can last a lifetime.

he made lonely night voyages in a little gilded boat. Herrenchiemsee, on an island in the lake of Chiemsee (the 'Bavarian Sea'), is a miniature Versailles, with similar gardens and architecture and mirrored hall, where candelit concerts are now staged.

Bavaria is the largest of the German states or *Länder*, and for more than seven centuries was a separate monarchy; it is not surprising that the locals regard themselves as a people apart. Germany has sometimes been likened to an upside-down Britain, which would make Bavaria a German Scotland. There is a similarity in the hospitable warmth of its highlanders, and the capital, Munich, has been likened to Edinburgh. However, its Oktoberfest – in which 240,000 gallons of beer are drunk in one

weekend – is hardly a parallel of Edinburgh's Festival. Furthermore, Bavaria is Catholic not Calvinist, and caters for the inner man with a versatility that astounds, and extends to the humblest *Gasthaus* or *Weinstube*. Nor is beer alone in being especially honoured. Bavaria abounds in festivals and local diversions – from the Christkindl Market at Nuremberg to the Children's Pageant at Dinkelsbühl, the Dance Festival at Kaufbeuren and, of course, the internationally famous Passion Play, presented every tenth year at Oberammergau.

The Black Forest is Bavaria's antidote to these rich festivities. Here the Romans 'heard the barbarians sing their songs on the other side of the Rhine, their language like the croaking of the raven,' and, venturing across, found 'the customs spontaneous and unbridled in this impenetrable wilderness of forest'. The wilderness is tamed now, and the locals have turned into an easy-going people who enjoy nothing better than to spend a hot summer's night in convivial feasting outdoors, then working off the calories with a morning hike up a mountain valley, among the buzzards and pheasants, deer and foxes, and countless sorts of butterfly.

Below the forest line are lush, wide meadows choc-a-bloc with contented cows, each carrying a bell with a different note; the older the cow, the bigger the bell. In September, they are brought down from the high pastures to winter in the lower valleys. Sometimes, in an isolated fold, you come upon a peasant's house with an enormous roof, built on a slope so steep that the front is a storey taller than the rear; a cuckoo clock ticks away in the dining room. Traditionally this is cuckoo clock country. Here the fabulous pop-out bird was first made in the middle of the 18th century and it remains the region's most famous product for tourists. At Schonach, there is a 23-foot spring with a 3-foot bird: the biggest cuckoo clock on earth. However, modern industries, highly sophisticated manufacturing of machinery and electronic goods have reduced the importance of these old crafts.

Unlike Upper Bavaria, where leather breeches, horn-buttoned jacket and felt hat with chamois' brush are still everyday wear for some older men, in the Black Forest the traditional costumes are only brought out on special occasions.

It is sobering to ponder the possibility that all this might soon be gone. There is more truth than hysteria in the warning slogan of the ecologists: 'Visit the German forests while they still exist.' *Waldsterben*, the dying forest syndrome, is proving an environmental disaster of far greater complexity than the poisoning of the Rhine. Figures for what was West Germany show that as much as 70 per cent of its woodland may be under immediate threat, and some fear that the country could be stripped bare in another 20 years, if nothing is done to reverse the process. The causes are clear: acid rain and other airborne pollutants from factories, power plants and car exhausts. The cure is not so certain. Studies show that an autobahn speed limit of 60mph would reduce exhaust emissions sufficiently to have some beneficial effect, but limitations of any kind naturally run into opposition from powerful industrial lobbies.

The Zwinger Museum, a Baroque masterpiece in Dresden, seemed lost for ever when it was bombed in February 1945. Beautifully restored in the 1950s, it houses a rich collection of porcelain, pewter and clocks. Raphael's Sistine Madonna, *painted in 1513, is the most famous picture in the Semper Gallery.*

Border guards look down impassively as crowds begin to dismantle the Berlin Wall in November 1989. Ever since 1961, the wall had divided the city and closed the last loophole between the East and the West.

A busy café on the wide terraces in front of the old Stock Exchange in the Naschmarkt, Leipzig. The Goethe monument in the distance reigns over 'little Paris', as the poet called his favourite town.

The other side of the mirror

On October 3, 1990 Germany was united once more. Nevertheless, once across what was once the frontier between the two Germanies, everything is the same and yet different: the same landscape, the same people, and yet it is another world.

Political upsets of the most spectacular kind have been a part of German history ever since Charlemagne's empire began to disintegrate in the 9th century. Only after the carnage of the Thirty Years War in the first half of the 17th century did Prussia begin to grow into the dominant power in the country. The climax of Prussian ambition came in 1871 when it united the entire country under an aristocracy whose imperial dreams were only shattered by the First World War. The inability of the old leadership to accept this reverse played an important part in the events that led to the Second World War, and the subsequent arbitrary division of the country.

Landscape and local architectural styles took no account of such a border. The Baltic shores, with their beaches, fishing ports and old towns of gabled houses, cone towers, red-brick walls and red tiles, are much as they were when Caspar David Friedrich painted them early in the 19th century. The island of Rügen, with its white cliffs, seagulls and wild geese, is likewise unchanged, and the same tourists (though minus their frock coats) seem to be watching the sea from the little cafés perched on the cliffs, just as they did 150 years ago. There is plenty of room to spread your towel on the beaches.

In the east of the country the houses may not be as neat and tidy as those in the west, or so carefully maintained, but those of historical interest are given every care. Wiek and Lubmin are old fishing villages with thatched cottages, most of them whitewashed, while some around the harbour are painted in bright colours. Rostock and Stralsund are old merchant cities which have been carefully restored; like Lübeck in the west of Germany and Gdansk in Poland, their wealth was founded on salt. There is still a sense of unity among these Hanseatic cities, members of the league formed in the Middle Ages to promote international trade by agreeing that no customs duty should be charged on goods in transit – a revolutionary concept at the time, but one which has become as commonplace as the duty-free shops at international airports.

Christmas in Germany

The many centuries of being chopped up into mini-states created an enduring regionalism, which can still be felt throughout Germany. The historical shifts have left their mark in other ways. Despite efforts at suppression under Communist rule, Germans in the east remain staunchly Protestant, in contrast to the Catholicism of much of the west; this was to be expected, since Wittenberg, the town where Martin Luther served as a priest and set the great Protestant Reformation in motion in the sixteenth century, lies in the heart of eastern Germany.

The Christmas period in Germany has various highlights: St Nicholas' Day on December 6, when the children are given small presents, and the first Sunday in Advent, when a wreath of pine branches tied with red ribbon is hung up and the first of four candles lit; the last candle is lit on the Sunday before Christmas, and on Christmas Eve the lights go up on the Christmas tree.

Germany has carefully preserved its religious architecture, notably the Romanesque Church of Gernrode and the Cistercian church at Chorin, a large and beautiful Gothic brick building, now noted for its concerts. Many of the smaller chapels, like the small oval structure of the French church of Schwedt on the Oder river are outstanding.

Historical links are cherished. Weimar honours Goethe and Schiller, and the patriarch of the

A small boy carries a mallet – his own contribution towards the destruction of the Berlin Wall which, together with a three-mile-wide zone of minefields and electrified fences, divided the Federal Republic of Germany from the German Democratic Republic.

Bach family, Johann Sebastian, is remembered at Eisenach. The Wartburg castle contains memories of Luther. Schiller, Herder, Liszt and Wagner are other great artists associated with Weimar, while Leipzig has a magnificent Bach archive. Some old crafts are very much alive: wood-carving and lace-making at Schneeberg, charming hand-made wooden toys at Seiffen, glass-blowing and beaded embroidery (called *passementerie*) in tne Erzgebirge Mountains. At Meissen, porcelain bearing the famous trademark of two blue crossed swords is made to a standard equal to that of any of the rare museum pieces. The State has set up various craft centres and folklore museums, and sponsored the restoration of old buildings like the town hall at Wernigerode and the water tower at Bautzen.

The 'Sorben' are a national minority in the Lander of Brandenburg, concentrated around Bautzen and Cottbus. They have their own theatre and Institute of Ethnology. Their dialect is kept alive through newspapers, magazines, the radio and books.

Youths wave the flag of a united Germany in front of the Brandenburg Gate, which lies at the western end of the Unter den Linden. At the time of the reunification celebrations in October 1990, the gate was missing its crowning 'Quadriga of Victory' – a statue of a chariot and horses – which had been damaged after the dismantling of the Berlin Wall at the end of 1990.

Charlotte's room

Before the Second World War the gently rolling country between Magdeburg and Berlin was the land of huge estates, and the way of life was almost feudal. The estates no longer exist, but the general impression remains one of infinite space, reinforced by huge fields of corn and barley and dark forests encircling icy lakes. The Communist government ruled what was once Prussia, the land ravaged, pacified and Christianised by the Teutonic knights, the source of German unity, and the home of high culture in the 18th and 19th centuries. In these uncompromising lands, which seem so typically German, there are some odd reminders of Italy. In southern Saxony, near the Czechoslovakian border, the forest is sprinkled with hunting lodges and temples to Diana where it is easy to imagine nymphs cavorting with the sylvan gods.

Dresden, incinerated by Allied incendiary bombs, has been carefully restored and is reminiscent of a Florentine townscape, with domed churches and tall-windowed palaces reflected in the Elbe. Here Canaletto was court painter to the ruler of Saxony, Augustus the Strong, and Friedrich Schiller, the master of German poetry and drama, wrote his major work, including the *Ode to Joy*, which forms the text for Beethoven's Ninth Symphony. And here the composers Weber and Wagner lived. In February 1945, waves of British and American bombers destroyed this unique city; the debate continues as to whether such an attack on a non-military target was really necessary. However, the continuing reconstruction efforts of the Germans are an extraordinary achievement. Their work on the Semper Opera is outstanding, recreated over ten years by artisans in exact accordance with the original plans. Still more remarkable is the reconstruction of the Zwinger Palace, which was considered the most beautiful Baroque building in the world when completed in 1728. It took craftsmen 19 years to duplicate all that was destroyed, including the Nymphs' Baths and the Carillon Pavilion, complete with its set of Dresden china bells. The Zwinger contains one of the world's great art collections; as well as Raphael's *Sistine Madonna* there are 12 paintings by Rembrandt, 16 by Rubens, five Tintorettos, and enough Canaletto portraits of Dresden in its prime to keep the restorers inspired towards further effort.

Thuringia is the heavily wooded heartland of German classical culture: here in Weimar, the middle-aged Goethe came to live and conduct long conversations with his friend Schiller. His house has been carefully restored as a museum. The city is immaculate, with many elegant houses restored. The traveller may even sleep in the very room where Charlotte, Goethe's life-long love, stayed as an elderly lady, when she came to see the man who had become known as 'the Olympian'. Strolling through the meadows beside the Ilm, and through the beech forests above Weimar, is a deeply emotional experience, for here in terrifying contrast is the death camp of Buchenwald (the name means 'beech wood'), which has been preserved as a monument to the Holocaust.

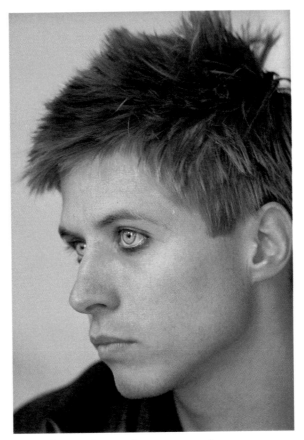

Berlin has a reputation as a youthful and stylish city. Fashions are important, and many that originate here spread west to other European cities.

A city after the apocalypse

Every Berliner will tell you that Berlin is not a city: it is a country. When you leave the airport you drive through suburbs, then through fields, lakes and woods, then more suburbs and finally, when you least expect it, you arrive at the Kurfürstendamm, a street with luxury shops and brilliant lighting, its theatres, restaurants and nightclubs, all dominated by the Gedächtniskirche, the bombed church that is a memorial to the dead of the Second World War. Even in its splintered state, Berlin covers an immense area, and every district is like a separate town, with its distinct flavour. Nothing could be more different than the Hansaviertel, a 48-architect vision of high-rise living that became a model for modern urban architecture, and Spandau, with its moated citadel hardly changed since its completion in 1594. The artificial grassy mounds like the Klamott, a rubbish dump of bomb debris, are a reminder of more recent events. War

Lively cafés with crowded terraces fill the Berlin pavements in the shadow of the Gedächtniskirche (Church of Remembrance). A modern tower was added to the bombed remains of the original building.

turned the place inside out. The old centre became the dividing line between two worlds, and has yet to be completely rebuilt.

In the centre of a large park is an imposing column made of umpteen cannon barrels captured in the course of 19th-century Prussian victories. Before the war the column stood outside the Parliament building; it looks a little odd in its splendid isolation, seen in the past as an appropriate symbol for this isolated outpost of the west, deep in East Germany. From the top of the Hilton Hotel, at the edge of the park, you can hear the roar of the animals in the Zoo and see the flag of the Federal Republic of Germany flying over the Brandenburg Gate.

To the east lies another part of city which is currently experiencing dramatic changes. To make the point clear, the Peace Goddess and her chariot atop the Brandenburg Gate have been turned around and now face eastward, up the majestic Unter den Linden, once a world-famous avenue that was to pre-war Berlin what Fifth Avenue or the Champs-Elysées are to New Yorkers or Parisians. Lined with restored palaces, it stretches as far as the tall Berlin Radio Tower.

Berlin's architectural legacy includes a large con-centration of neo-classical palaces and a few blocks of small, quaint houses which form the oldest part of the city. It also has Museum Island on the Spree, where the treasures of the magnificent Pergamon Museum are worth seeing on any visit to Berlin. They include a street of ancient Babylon and the awesome Pergamon Altar, one of the Seven Wonders of the ancient world, unearthed and brought stone by stone from Turkey.

New districts are gradually being added to Berlin. The Alexanderplatz, before the war a popular and lively square that is remembered in post-war West German novels and films, is now flanked by Karl-Marx Allee, a monumental avenue lined with high-rise blocks in the most brutal Stalinist style.

Berliners are proud of their cultural heritage. A small theatre houses the Berliner Ensemble. This world-famous group of players is dedicated to per-forming the plays and songs of Bertold Brecht, whose lyrics, set to the harsh, strident music of Kurt Weill, are as popular as ever. They seem perfectly to capture the spirit of the Berliner: dry, witty and sharp-tongued.

Of course, the city is divided no longer. Berlin is a special place for all Germans: once the symbol of a broken dream, it is now the cradle of a new Utopia.

Away from the big seaside resorts, the German beaches retain an old-fashioned charm. The wind is so strong that bathers shelter in these quaint wicker chairs.

Switzerland

Beneath the waters of the lake of Neuchâtel lie the remains of
a prehistoric village. After careful study, archaeologists came to a startling
conclusion. None of the 3000-year-old huts was larger than the rest, nor was
there any suggestion of a palace or temple, or any indications of a hierarchy.
Yet the buildings were arranged according to a precise plan that implied a
high level of organisation. As far back as research can go, however deeply
the Swiss spirit is studied, an innate need for order is apparent.
No nation on earth is more meticulous, or has demonstrated
more clearly its deep desire for social harmony.

These huts in the Valais are perched precariously on a little shelf below a glacier. The first snows have whitened the heights above the Val d'Herens. It is time to make repairs before winter comes.

Clock-making is a Swiss tradition. Long before the Dutchman Huyghens invented the coiled spring, the Swiss knew how to put together complicated mechanisms that showed the hour and the signs of the zodiac and set small figures in motion, as here in Berne's 460-year-old Zytgloggeturm, or Clock Tower.

Previous page: *The national flag and banners of the Swiss cantons flying on the Mont Blanc bridge. Geneva mounts this display during holidays and festivals.*

A Land of Peace and Prosperity

Switzerland is a small country of startling scenic beauty, with mountain, lake and river all in such perfect proportion that they seem to have been created to a plan. Nowhere has nature been so prodigal with grandiose effect from glacier, chasm, peak and gorge. The softness of the summer climate is countered by the severity of winter, and the people have adapted to every difficulty in learning to live with what early 19th-century romantics called 'these terrible mountains'. Switzerland is both wild fantasy, and a model of organisation: it is order within disorder. Snow, chalets, edelweiss and cuckoo clocks – so complete and firmly fixed is its popular image that millions who have never been there feel they know it well. This is both an advantage and a disadvantage, for the Swiss find themselves having to live up to an idealised concept, a vision distilled from the rapture of several generations of poets, painters, musicians and travel agents.

Everyone knows of Switzerland as a land of mountains, but there is also the central plateau, the Mittelland (middle land), held vice-like between the heavily wooded Jura and the Alps. Between these ranges, a web of high-tension electricity cables is slung across hills and valleys to converge on the big urban centres, Zurich and Winterthur, Basel, Berne and Geneva, all sited on lake shores where there is some flat ground to allow for expansion. Though a plateau in Swiss terms, the Mittelland is more of a sloping ditch, which only 100 years ago was choked by debris-bearing glaciers churning down from the Alps. Now that the ice fields have diminished in size as melting has occurred, the area is a fertile, undulating region of rivers and lakes, and it is here that two-thirds of the population live, most of them employed in industry.

So much for the assumption that Switzerland produces nothing but cheese and chocolate, clocks and musical boxes, without a smoke-stack in sight – yet it is remarkably adroit at disguising or dispelling all that disfigures or displeases. A drive through the Appenzell or Gruyère districts reveals a gentle countryside dappled with meadows, hop fields, copses and orchards, and well populated by contented-looking cows. There is a strong smell of manure everywhere, yet by some miracle known only to the Swiss no cow pats can be seen; seemingly, they are immediately removed, just like anything else that might be regarded as objectionable or out of place. This idyll is a major achievement of the Swiss. Almost anywhere else, such an isolated plateau at an average altitude of 2500 feet would certainly have been left well alone.

This armailli *(cowman) of Gruyère has cultivated a beard to rival the splendour of his jacket, which is embroidered with the traditional edelweiss.*

*The best known Alpine flower, the edelweiss (*Leartopodium alpinum*) flourishes on chalky slopes. A high-altitude plant, sometimes called immortal because it can be dried and keeps so easily, it is one of the symbols of Switzerland.*

High up on the mountain

The mountains are near enough: the highest in Europe, and so approachable that signposts mark the *Wanderweg* (footpaths) along which the Swiss set out in force on Sundays, whole families at a time, alpenstocks in hand, rucksacks on their backs, to climb to the foot of a glacier where they will find a hut of the Swiss Alpine Club, flying the familiar white cross on its red background. Wild streams tumble down from the glaciers to water the dark pines, which lend a touch of gloom to the ravines bottomed by lakes left over from the last ice age. The fulcrum of the Swiss Alps is the St Gotthard massif, western Europe's watershed, and its water-tower too, for it is the source of the Rhine and Rhône, and supplies the Po and Danube besides. The road that was forced through the St Gotthard Pass some time after the 13th century was vital to securing Swiss independence and nationhood.

A woman of Gruyère. Her plaits are threaded with black ribbons that are tied under her chin, and the gold threads on her pleated bodice reflect the fairness of her hair. Such old-fashioned elegance is still to be found in the canton of Fribourg.

There are many variations to the basic theme: you cannot confuse a valley in the Valais, or the Bernese Oberland, with a valley in the Grisons, or the Tessin; there is something more exotic about the Grisons, and a smiling warmth about the Oberland. Conditions are variable hour to hour, day to day, valley to valley, and at different levels of the same valley. During summer, local winds called *brises* are caused by air moving up the rock corridors, only to reverse direction suddenly and set temperatures plunging; in winter, the treacherous *Föhn* wind can send dry hot air tumbling over the crests and cause devastating avalanches and forest fires, yet it also clears the spring pastures of snow and allows vines and other Mediterranean vegetation to grow in some valleys.

'It's all due to the climate' – those who try to explain such a complex country in this way overlook the skill with which the Swiss have adapted their environment. Enormous amounts of courage and endurance have gone into turning so much rugged rock into assorted aspects of paradise. The neat appearance of many a lower slope is achieved by careful cropping and the greenness of the Valais is a tribute to dogged Swiss ingenuity in creating a water supply where the forces of nature create enormous problems. For the Valais is in the depths of a rain shadow, and the steep gradients rule out normal irrigation methods. The solution was a network of *bisses* (water snakes), more than 1200 miles of pipes and aqueducts, which run from the melting base of the glaciers. The *bisses* plunge down mountainsides, and are sometimes giddily suspended hundreds of feet over a ravine or a gorge. Maintaining such a water supply, and organising its careful distribution

Guarda, above the river En (or Inn), is a celebration of local architecture: walls at unexpected angles, windows and other details picked out against a white or pink background reminiscent of neighbouring Italy.

Folk singers in Gruyère. Men stand with their glasses of white wine, in conversation with the women in their lace bonnets. Gruyère is a picture-postcard dream, tucked within ramparts on top of a rocky crag. It is closed to traffic, but not to tourist invasion.

among the villages, helps to sustain a powerful social cohesion; in spring, when the sluices are opened, religious services are held and blessings sought, even though modern pumping stations now supplement the rustic supply lines.

A Swiss mountain is rarely what it seems; it is all too likely to have a massive hydro-electric generator, or an army fort, built deep inside it, for it is policy to augment the country's formidable natural defences with carefully hidden military strong-points, and it is also policy to construct power plants in a way that does not disturb the habitat. Such undertakings are typical of Swiss logic – if you want to live in peace, you must arm to protect yourself; if you value nature, you must safeguard it, if necessary by altering it. The Swiss are tough on themselves.

Much of Switzerland is man-made beauty – nature's gifts turned to their best advantage – and there are those who regard the result as too elaborate, too chocolate box, with one too many mountains scaled by ski lifts, and with too comfortable a hotel on the top. But this is to criticise the Swiss for being Swiss, and to scold them for treating their tourists so well. The proprietor of the most remote mountain inn would be deeply shamed if he could not produce exactly the right beer or cheese to order. For years, there were jokes about the Swiss vacuum-cleaning their roads, until one day a large electric machine was spotted doing precisely that. In Switzerland, road-sweepers and dustmen look smarter than the waiters in some other countries.

Interior of a house in Guarda. The ceiling is vaulted in the Italian manner, while the antique pine furniture is local. Neatness is typical of the Engadine, where home-owners are obsessively house-proud.

Chalet culture

For proof of the indomitable will of the Swiss, look to their homes; scattered over the steepest mountain slopes, they strike a welcoming note in the wildest settings where, among the rock falls and avalanches, families as isolated as Robinson Crusoe plant crops on slopes whose near 45-degree angles barely give a footing to the heavy-booted children with milk churns balanced on their backs, or to the wife gone to break the morning ice on the mountain spring. You have to be physically as well as mentally strong in these parts. To discover the character of these people examine their houses, so comfortable and so polished that the smell of pine and wax is the first thing that comes out to greet you.

One particular style, the *Schali*, or chalet, of the Bernese Oberland, has in this century come to typify the Swiss house in the eyes of the world, but it is only one in a rich variety of designs developed over the centuries. It is not only the materials available that create the differences between the styles of the Jura and the Grisons, and between Toggenburg and Tessin (Ticino): historical considerations and skills also affect building techniques, and determine that around Berne they prefer to build in wood what in the Engadine is likely to be of stone.

The chalet is properly built of pine, has a low-pitched roof to hold the snow as insulation, and carved balconies at each storey; in the high pastures, it will be of humbler construction, and roofed with wooden shingles weighted down by stones. In the Valais they build taller, plainer, and in larch. Since this is a windy region in which fire is a constant threat, there is an attached kitchen block of brick. Next to the main building is the *raccord*, or *mazot*, a miniature chalet perched on piles, and used to store grain and valuables such as property deeds, so that they are safe from the rats. They are a practical folk in the Valais. 'It's not like the other side, where you'd think they were living in a forest of geraniums,' they say with undisguised disdain. 'The other side' is the other side of the Jungfrau, in the Oberland, where every corner carries a carved animal or monster, and every beam bears a coat of arms, with maybe a verse from the Bible as a finishing touch. This is the classic chalet of doll's house delight, its outside walls hung with hunting trophies, and its balconies bright with plants – geraniums in particular.

A steep roof and weatherboarding to protect the

A doorway in Guarda. The door is carved in a linen-fold pattern seen in other Alpine valleys, but the etched wall decorations, called sgraffiti, *are unique to the Engadine and carry a government preservation order.*

The Unterwald is the historical and geographical heartland of the Helvetian federation. Here, tradition rules. Each spring the shepherds pile cooking utensils, mattresses and other essentials on old carts to spend their summer in the mountains.

A chalet in Leysin, a sunny spot high up in the mountains. The winter supply of wood is piled high on the ground floor.

with a fusion of chalet and Italian elements that delights in its freedom of line and expression. The white walls of these Engadine houses are decorated with intricate designs using a process known as *sgrafitto*, and have small, irregularly placed windows whose thick casements widen outwards, and are sometimes enclosed in richly decorated wrought iron grilles. A paved ramp leads up to a double door, with panels that can be opened singly, or altogether to admit a vehicle into the *suler*, a covered court which is the centre of family activity.

This stylistic diversity is no more remarkable than the cultural and environmental diversity, with its different demands every few miles. A style appropriate for one valley is likely to be so unsuitable as to be unthinkable in the next, and practicality lies behind much that the tourist finds charming. The houses of the Engadine and Grisons are big enough for two or three families to share, and are ideal for the needs of the locality, just as the relationship of the Appenzeller with his cattle determines design

Carving a water trough. From splendid civic stone monument to simple tap and trough in a tiny village square, a fountain is a part of every Swiss community.

shuttered windows distinguishes the style around Lucerne; there the entrance is high above ground, and reached by an outdoor stairway. In rainy Appenzell, near Lake Constance in the north-east, wooden shingles, laid like fish scales, cover the entire façade. In Emmental, of cheese fame, the dominant feature is a huge roof, reaching down like a hood at the sides; some ambitious owners replace this with a majestic timber arch. The wine-growers of the Jura build low, and in brick, while Italian influence is strong in the Ticino Alps, where the thickly walled homes are mostly of stone. The transalpine corridor of the dry, sunny En (Inn) Valley in the Grisons has come up in that dairying region, where even crockery and leather goods are emblazoned with images of cows; here the cowshed is attached to the house, with cheerful yellow walls and carved panelled doors, usually bright red, to proclaim its importance. But this much is common: from the flagstones of an Engadine *suler* to the shingles on a snow-line chalet, every element of every home is immaculately maintained, for the care that the Swiss put into their homes springs from a determination to turn each into a private view of paradise.

It is an intensely private view, for communities were self-sustaining and isolated for long stretches of the year until well into the 19th century. It is said that early last century the inhabitants of Ernen in the Valais refused the use of their gallows for the execu-

tion of a murderer from a neighbouring village. 'Sorry,' they said, 'but these gallows are for us and for our children.' Nidwalden has still not forgiven Obwalden for failing to join the fight against Napoleon, and the Hungarian humorist George Mikes tells the story of a Zurich industrialist who did not like to employ anyone from Appenzell because the people there were 'impertinent and mean', or anyone from Grisons because they were 'too unreliable', or St Gallen ('a lazy lot'), or Berne ('slow-witted'), or Lucerne ('spoilt by tourism'), and who even dismissed his own son when he married a girl from Zug, because the people of Zug (12 miles away) were 'petty and calculating'. Then there was the Basel businessman who confided, 'I do not hate the Zurichers. I only despise them.'

Making Gruyère cheese in the Leysin mountains. Most Swiss cheese production is a highly commercial operation, but people still occasionally resort to the old ways.

All of this has the effect of making Switzerland seem very much bigger than it is, for how can so many differences be packed into a nation just half the size of Scotland? Mikes considered 'healthy detestation of one another' to be the secret of the success of Swiss democracy and neutrality, since, he argued, it had led people to fall back upon 'the shining democratic virtue of tolerance'. Certainly, no amount of mutual antagonism does any harm to the fierce patriotism that all of them share.

The solid Swiss citizen

In Swiss cities there are no princely palaces, but comfortable houses, each making its individual contribution. To own your own house marks a certain advance in the social scale, which is both a matter of personal pride and a reason to require a measure of respect from others. Extravagance and ostentation are to be avoided at all costs: sober elegance is the keynote, with even a touch of austerity commensurate with the subtle display of wealth. Geneva, Lucerne, Neuchâtel, Berne, Zurich, Basel or Schaffhausen: they all share this sense of well-being, of solid comfort so different from the spirit of cathedral-crowned cities like Seville, Milan or Chartres. What luxury there is, is rooted securely in the past: in the fountains decorated with grotesque figures, or men in armour waving a banner bearing the city's coat of arms; in German-speaking Switzerland, such items are the centrepiece of town squares. Old houses around the square are painted with allegorical themes, or stories from the Bible, always with a moral lesson that served as an excuse for a degree of display which would otherwise have raised eyebrows. In these respectable streets filled with businessmen, traders and bankers – solid burghers to a man – there are few multi-millionaires, but there are even fewer paupers. Wealth is usually an accumulation of several generations' effort, and it is not to be squandered; there is no dishonour in the rich travelling second-class, and even the President of the Swiss Republic might be seen in a bus queue.

A near-obsessive cleanliness is the most visible

Gruyère cheese maturing. The cheeseman has to turn the huge 'wheels' regularly. It is hard work, for each cheese weighs 100 pounds. Quality is strictly controlled, and each cheese is stamped with its place of origin.

manifestation of a philosophy of life that has sustained the Swiss through 700 years since the men of the future cantons of Schwyz, Uri and Nidwalden created the Swiss Confederation with a pledge 'to succour each other with mutual help and advice and with all their might'. The emphasis was on 'mutual', and since that time Swiss society has been committed to an egalitarian ideal, attended by a deep sense of discipline and an inclination for extreme respectability. A Swiss pedestrian is likely to wait for a street-light to turn green before crossing, even when no vehicle is in sight. Politeness can also become obsessive. Expressions of gratitude are forever being exchanged, and the greeting 'Grütsi' is offered to all and sundry; Swiss-watcher George Mikes even claims to have met a cow that refused to let him pass until he had said 'Grütsi', whereupon 'she nodded to me seriously and walked on'.

It was their determination to iron out social differences that made the Swiss refuse to grant Berne the title of capital, although it performs this function. When roads had to be built, buses were given preference over private cars. Everyone must give priority to the buttercup-yellow vehicles of the excellent Swiss postal bus service, with hunting horn logo painted on their sides and three-tone klaxon herald-

ing their approach. Some people declare that the only place where Swiss conformism has not been able to impose its will is in the cemetery. Visit a village graveyard and see how much care is lavished on the family plot. Some of these gardens of the dead are such horticultural triumphs that it is hard to know if the flower displays demonstrate an immoderate affection for the departed, or an almost indecent obsession with gardening.

Yet the community approach does not get in the way of private enterprise. When other state-owned airlines are nose-diving into debt, it may be surprising to learn that proud and efficient Swissair is two-thirds privately owned and has no direct government subsidy. Again, there are almost a hundred private railways operating in support of the state network with its crack expresses. They provide an intricate service to otherwise inaccessible places that is unique in the world. The organisation that has gone into the railways is almost as impressive as the engineering required to tunnel the Simplon, St Gotthard and Lotschberg, or claw up the one-in-two gradient of Mount Pilatus, or design routes that curl so gracefully in and out of mountains and suddenly dive out of the clouds to reveal a valley full of vineyards, or fields of wild narcissi. Local pride, more than a desire for profit, was the spur to many a spur line. The story is told of the businessman who financed the building of a funicular railway to his home village, simply because it did not have one; his only stipulation was that he and his family were to ride free.

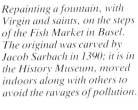

Repainting a fountain, with Virgin and saints, on the steps of the Fish Market in Basel. The original was carved by Jacob Sarbach in 1390; it is in the History Museum, moved indoors along with others to avoid the ravages of pollution.

Switzerland is the land of the citizen-soldier, and on Sundays many armed civilians head for the firing range. The weapons, official issue, are kept at home.

Cheese, watches, hotels and banks

The only excess which the Swiss allow themselves is hard work. They start early and finish late, and while they expect to be well-paid they consider it their duty to give value for money. Mountain people everywhere tend to be conservative, and dogged rather than nimble-minded; the Swiss themselves make jokes about the Bernese being slow, which the Bernese say is just as well for Switzerland, and why the capital is best sited in sensible, methodical Berne. These characteristics are allied to a fascination with novelty comparable to that of the Americans: the Swiss will try anything new, and were consequently among the first into computers and automation and similar innovations.

The Swiss economy makes full use of this in concentrating upon a few things that come naturally.

Take Gruyère cheese, a leading export of unsurpassed quality, as the local television stations never tire of reminding their viewers. It starts as grass, which is tended as carefully as an English lawn. Then come the cows, each wearing a heavy bell, which surely must encourage them to browse seriously rather than be deafened every time they raise their heads. Above Verbier, about 140 miles of 'lacto-ducts' have been built to speed the product from alpine pasture to dairies where conditions are as clinical as those of a hospital; if you doubt this, visit the plant at Gruyère, where workers dressed in white carry out their work like surgeons behind glass and chromium panels.

Fine watches and precision instruments have long been the hallmark of Swiss technical skill. The stern 16th-century religious reformer John Calvin forced Swiss goldsmiths to turn to clock-making when he condemned crosses and chalices as works of the

A close-up of life in the Omega factory: watch manufacture demands skilled craftsmanship, and precision must be accurate to 1/10,000th of an inch.

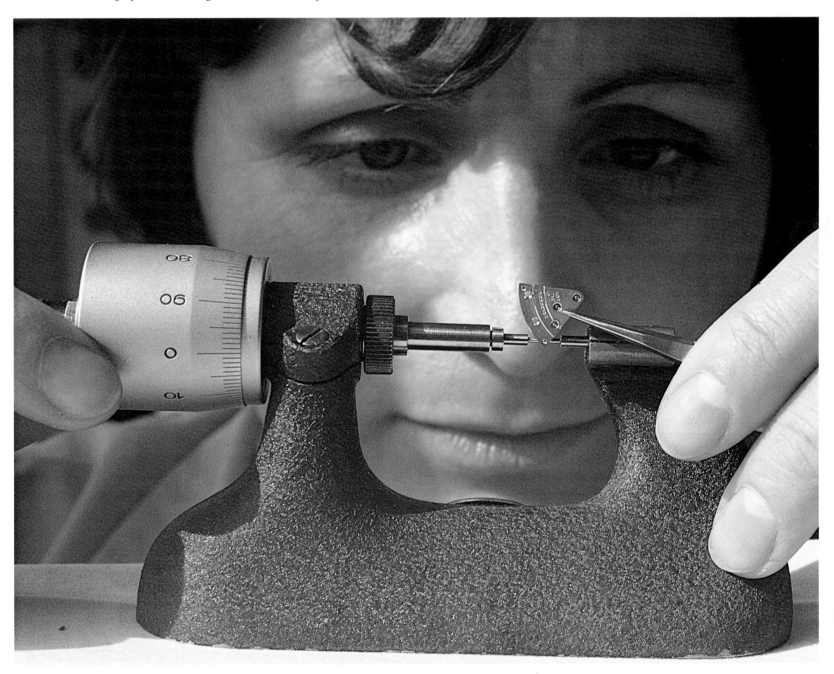

Devil, but a 17th-century handyman named Daniel Jean-Richard is honoured as Father of the Swiss watch. The story goes that an English horse-dealer, travelling in the Jura in 1679, found that his watch had stopped. He went to see Jean-Richard, who had never before clapped eyes on this new-fangled invention, but assured the Englishman that he could fix it. During the night, Jean-Richard not only took the watch to pieces and repaired it, but made a complete set of drawings of the movement. Within a few years, he had set up Switzerland's first watch factory. Most of the watch-making industry is still concentrated in the Jura. The response to intense competition from Japan and elsewhere has been a search for perfection; the precision-tolerance for working parts is now 1/400th of a millimetre – 1/10,000th of an inch. All sorts of machinery, from scientific and optical instruments to locomotive and ship turbines, enjoy the same reputation for precision and reliability, and their manufacture is Switzerland's major industry.

Hotel-keeping as a profession was virtually invented in Switzerland, where the national attributes of cleanliness and diligence were just the qualities needed; farmer to hotel executive remains a natural progression. The first establishment was opened at Rigi-Kulm in 1816, and had 294 guests in its first year. Others opened at Paulhorn in 1832, and at Pilatus and Riffleberg in the 1850s, but again it was the English who provided the spur to greatness.

Tourism was concentrated around the lakes until an English party, persuaded in 1864 to winter at the Kulm hotel, invented the winter sports holiday, and Edward Whymper popularised mountaineering when he conquered the Matterhorn a few months later. Thereupon Queen Victoria, on a donkey, conquered Mount Pilatus, and there was no looking back. Skiing took a little longer; even though it had been known in Scandinavia for 6000 years, 'plank-hopping' was viewed with disdain, and one of the first to try it seriously, and write about it, was Sir Arthur Conan Doyle in 1885. The first downhill race was not staged until 1911, with the boom following in the 1920s. By the end of the 1930s there were more than 100 ski resorts. Swiss tourism generated famous dynasties of hoteliers, including the Seilars from Zermatt and the Badrutts of St Moritz, and César Ritz teamed with chef Auguste Escoffier to blaze a trail of gastronomic glory from Lucerne to London. While French cuisine remains the major influence, Swiss master chefs are now prized around the world, their trustworthy reputation crowning their quality as cooks.

Just as hotel ownership represents the dream of many a Swiss farmer, so banking fires the ambitions of every Swiss businessman; there is nothing like visions of secret wealth, and the reputation of the 'gnomes of Zurich', to quicken his pulse. There is a saying: 'If you see a banker jump out of a window, jump after him. There's bound to be some profit

The coat of arms adopted by the Helvetian Confederation, a white cross on a red ground, began as the emblem of the canton of Schwyz, one of the Waldstatten *(Forest States) that united to gain their independence of the ruling Habsburg family in 1291.*

On the Spitalgasse, in the heart of Berne, flags are put out on every possible occasion. The bright colours of national emblem, city banner and standards of the professional guilds strike vivid notes against the buildings.

in it.' Some people complain that the Swiss love money too much, but it would be more accurate to say that they revere it; as has been noted, to squander money is to commit a sin in Switzerland, so there is a disinclination to throw it about. Their businessmen perpetually amaze by fussing over a few francs, even while they are dealing adroitly with millions. To quote George Mikes again: 'The whole world loves the Swiss franc, but only the Swiss adore the Swiss centime.' This makes for a tight-fisted reputation, but with it comes a reputation for unsurpassed honesty.

Four languages and one people

Language is another eccentricity of the Swiss, which throws up barriers as tall as their mountains. The country is divided into three language areas, or more properly four, which for practical purposes become five, six, seven and not even linguists can be sure of the precise number of local variations which render hazardous any vocal venture beyond a yodel.

The problem began with the break-up of the Roman Empire, whereupon Germanic and Gallic tribes battled each other to a standstill at the River Sarine (Saane), which to this day is the dividing line between German-speaking and French-speaking Switzerland. About two-thirds of Swiss are classified as German-speaking, 18 per cent French-speaking, and 12 per cent in the south-west are Italian-speaking, but there the complications just begin. The spoken German of Switzerland is Schwitzerdeutsch, derived from an ancient tribal dialect, and likened by its critics (the actual Germans foremost among them) to gargling during a bad attack of tonsillitis. It is the reason why many a ravishing Swiss miss is under advice from her parents to smile, but say nothing. Moreover, every district has its own version of Schwitzerdeutsch, so everyone stands out as a 'foreigner' within a few miles of his home town or village.

The French-speaking Swiss do not like to learn German, and regard Schwitzerdeutsch as a return to barbarism; while the Italian Swiss have little inclination to learn either French or German. However, the industrious German-speaking Swiss travel more readily, and will try French, or Italian, which has

To imagine Zurich without banks would be impossible. To its citizens banking is a vocation, a battleground and a setting for the highest individual achievement in business life.

tended to mangle language even further. Something akin to a Swiss ideal exists in the Sarine Valley towns of Bienne (Biel) and Fribourg (Frieburg), where it is common to hear animated conversations in which one person is speaking French and the other Schwitzerdeutsch. Swiss diligence has been applied to the commercial aspects of trilingualism, and all commodities are clearly marked '*Milch/lait/latte*', and so on, though the depths of the cultural cauldron become apparent with a product like disposable nappies: *lange à jeter* to the French Swiss, *Wegwerfwindeln* to the German Swiss, and *pannolini da gettar via dopo l'uso* to the Italian Swiss!

Moreover, there is yet a further complication – again thanks to the Romans, whose legionaries spoke a kind of Cockney Latin that some mountain folk still use today. This is Romansch, a relic of the Ancient Roman province of Rhaetia, spoken by about 50,000 people in the mountains of Ticino and the Grisons, but again divided into five mutually unintelligible dialects; even this fractured 0.8 per cent of the population is provided with some radio and television programming. The Rhaeto-Romansch celebrate their New Year on March 1, and can claim one significant contribution to history: it was Rhaetian legionaries who crucified Jesus.

It takes democracy of a high order to bind together such a muddle, and the Swiss were exercising the democratic vote (but for men only) hundreds of years before the rest of Europe emerged from feudalism. The Swiss constitution is similar to that of the United States, with each of the 23 cantons a little republic in charge of its own internal affairs, such as education, health and police, and exacting its own taxes. In three of the cantons, Appenzell, Glaris and Unterwald, vestiges survive of the original system of direct democracy, when men gathered, sword in hand, at open-air assemblies called *Landsgemeinden*. These 'votings' by a show of hands take place in the spring and are accompanied by ritual processions and patriotic singing, which makes them an irresistible attraction for hordes of sightseers and for the television cameras.

Federal and cantonal elections are held every four years. There is a National Council and a States Council, which is an upper house much like the US Senate, and a seven-member executive Federal Council, with the presidency rotating annually. That hardly anyone ever hears of the President of Switzerland is seen as one of the glories of a system of which the Swiss are inordinately proud. 'In our country everyone is in control and everything runs smoothly,' they insist in their sing-song accents. It is the cherished right of any citizen to initiate legislation by collecting signatures for a referendum, to which the Government must submit, but the system is so based on proportional representation, and on finely tuned balance, that most controversial decisions get settled by committees. 'Everything is beautifully dull, and I really do mean beautifully,' wrote George Mikes in his *Switzerland for Beginners*.

This country has worked beautifully for hundreds of years, though the future may be harder to handle. Switzerland is short of manpower, and hundreds of thousands of imported *Gastarbeiter* (guest workers) have formed an under-class, doing the dirty jobs and yet resented for supposedly causing *Uberfremdung* (diluting the country's national character). Young people increasingly fret over the bland certainties of their elders, and Zurich has a drug problem: a horrendous thing to bear for citizens who have traditionally regarded even bourgeois Geneva as dangerously racy. There is also the matter of women, who only gained the Federal vote in 1971 and who still cannot vote in local elections in part of Appenzell, where the men wear rings in the right ear, and smoke their decorated *lendeauerli* pipes upside down, and like things to stay the way they are. So far, feminism has not seriously challenged the male chauvinism of the Alps.

Swiss resorts are unparalleled in their combination of sport and luxury. In St Moritz, gold gleams from every window in the Via Arona. At Zermatt, boutiques sell crampons for climbing the Matterhorn as well as haute couture *dresses and accessories.*

Crossbows at the ready

At times everyday Swiss life seems trapped in tradition, for the simplest activies have a tendency to become ritualised. Take the life of the cowman. Swiss cows summer in the mountains and winter in the valleys, and though nothing could be more commonplace, their seasonal migrations are surrounded by ceremonial. Not only do the cows wear heavy and sonorous bronze bells for the journey, but each animal is bedecked in flowers and ribbons; endless files of them can be seen in late May and early June, accompanied by herdsmen burdened by all that they need for a summer on the high pasture (the 'alp'), even including huge cheese boilers. The end of the journey is celebrated with the *ranz*, or cow fight to decide who will be queen of the herd and wear the giant bell of office. Even the frantic activity of high summer is not allowed to mar the midsummer festival, when friends and relatives climb up from the valleys, and calves and cheeses are distributed. In the Gruyère region, the *armailli* or cowman still wears the traditional embroidered waistcoat, the *bredzon*, a shirt which leaves the arms bare for stirring the curds in the cheese vats, and the *capette*, a small cap embroidered with edelweiss. In Appenzell the *armaillis* wear short yellow trousers, a brightly embroidered waistcoat, a shirt with puff sleeves and a little straw cap edged with embroidered velvet.

Similar traditions apply to reapers and winegrowers; in fact, to workers of all kinds. In the Oberland, the peasants wear chamois leather shorts and flowered braces. In the Valais, the women go out to reap in ankle-length skirts, a handkerchief round their necks and their heads protected by wide straw

hats with the brim tied down with ribbons. For processions, fine silk aprons and the *mandzon*, a plain, long-sleeved jacket, are taken out of the painted wooden cupboards, along with lace bonnets with black felt crowns. In the Jura, and around Geneva, the end of the harvest marks the start of the

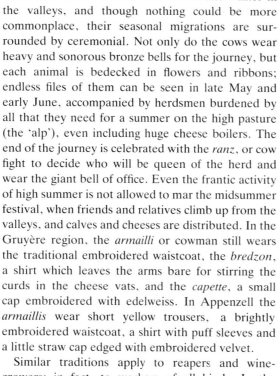

The Wine-growers' Festival in romantic Vevey is an unrestrained carnival. But it is only held every quarter-century, the last in 1977.

Clowns playing the flute during the carnival in Basel. During the first Monday in Lent a sense of gaiety verging on madness sweeps over this cosmopolitan centre of commerce.

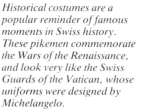

Historical costumes are a popular reminder of famous moments in Swiss history. These pikemen commemorate the Wars of the Renaissance, and look very like the Swiss Guards of the Vatican, whose uniforms were designed by Michelangelo.

wine festival, but at Vevey, among the vineyards of the Lavaux, the prodigious *Fête des Vignerons* (wine-growers' festival) is held only every 25 years.

In towns and cities, events like the carnival of Basel or the International Festival of Barrel Organs at Thun are further excuse for bringing out old costumes that can stand comparison with the most elaborate fancy dress. No festival worthy of the name takes place without the oompah-pah of a rustic orchestra, playing tunes originally used for clog dancing, and few Swiss avoid recruitment into some sort of band. In the mountains they rarely play the

alpenhorn, except for tourists, though it may still be heard in its natural state in Emmental, along with the occasional yodel.

Some festivals are more civic and patriotic. For the Knabenschissen in Zurich, people don old-fashioned uniform and parade behind a military band. And on the national day all of Switzerland celebrates the anniversary of the Founding Pact signed by the men of Uri, Schwyz and Unterwald on August 1, 1291. The night before, a performance of Schiller's play *Wilhelm Tell* is given at Interlaken to commemorate the legendary national hero, condemned by the Austrian tyrant Gessler to the famous test of shooting an apple placed on his son's head (which he accomplished, later shooting the tyrant as well).

The celebrations would not be complete without a shooting contest, for in Switzerland shooting is a national sport. Once upon a time the crossbow, as used by William Tell (and modern chamois hunters), was the weapon of choice, but nowadays army rifles are more common. Every fit adult male has to be ready for instant mobilisation, and keeps his army rifle at home. Target practice is both a pleasure and a duty, and on Sundays the hills are alive to the sound of rifle-fire after church services. Here we come to the crux of the Swiss experience, for Switzerland, host of peace conferences, home of the Red Cross, and a land so neutral that it has even declined to join the United Nations, is one of the most militarised nations of Europe. Like every Swiss attitude, this one goes back a long way: to 1515, when a Swiss force of 20,000 was defeated by a French and Venetian army of 60,000, equipped with the latest artillery. Numbers never bothered the Swiss much, but the prospect of a costly arms race did, so they formally renounced all territorial ambition and took their leave of the European power struggle. Instead, they set about turning a profit from other people's wars, to which they contributed regiments of hired mercenaries whose bravery and dedication to their employers became legendary; it is not for nothing that to this day the Pope's Vatican guards are Swiss.

Switzerland was confirmed as a neutral state in the 1648 treaty that ended the Thirty Years' War (in which it had avoided involvement), and, despite the efforts of Napoleon, it has remained so ever since. Its 'land of mercy' image was bolstered by the First World War, when it organised Red Cross units and provided sanctuary for wounded escapees and prisoners of war. Geneva then became the home of the League of Nations, with its mandate to end all wars, but when the Nazis destroyed that dream all the Swiss passes were fully manned and ready to be defended to the death, even before Britain had declared war on Germany. With the passes certain to be blown, and the invaders' losses inordinate, there was no point to invasion.

It takes a very secure government, and a society of extraordinary civility, to permit the entire population to stay armed at all times. In Switzerland they may only hand in their guns at the age of 50, or 55 in the case of officers. By that time the weapon will have acquired a remarkable sheen, for it is in the nature of the Swiss *Hausfrau* to polish, and to polish regularly. The Swiss Army probably has the most highly polished guns in the world.

The chamois is the goat-like antelope of the Alps. William Tell, the national hero, was a chamois hunter when not shooting apples off heads.

Snow on a slope has been the making of many a Swiss fortune since the English tumbled to its delights in the 1860s. Lately, cross-country skiing has become popular. This loipe, *or track, is at Zernez, just outside the Swiss National Park.*

Austria

The name conjures up images of waltzes in the Vienna Woods,
jolly Tyroleans bounding about their mountains, a sleigh with tinkling bells
dashing over blue-white snow, comfortable matrons seated before piles
of cream cakes, the Hofburg Palace, the White Horse Inn and Mayerling,
the child Mozart and the ageing Emperor Franz Joseph, a fabulous past
. . . and there the images end, for the present is something
that the Austrians are still working on.

A sturdy Tyrolean in a traditional folk festival outfit strides through a village in the Alps. Although foreigners think of skiing as the country's national sport, the Austrian is more likely to be fond of mountaineering, or hiking along some solitary path that leads to one of the many hospitable mountain retreats.

Previous page: *A girl of the Tyrol. The people here feel more than just a desire to dress up occasionally in traditional costume: it is a deeply felt affection for old habits and customs passed down through the generations.*

The Heart of the Alps

Austria is actually more alpine than Switzerland (71 per cent as opposed to 62 per cent) and its most western *Land* (federated province) is entirely cut off from the rest of the country by the Lechtaler Alps. This is the Vorarlberg (it means 'in front of the Arlberg'), a knob of territory wedged between Germany and Switzerland, where the people share the Germanic background of their neighbours and speak a brand of German more akin to Schwytzerdeutsch than to the Viennese *Dialekt*. Even the power from their dams goes largely to Germany.

A local legend disputes the claims of Mount Ararat, and maintains that it was here, in the Vorarlberg, that Noah's Ark came to rest after the flood. The Viennese may mock them for their isolation and make jokes about their stinginess, but the Vorarlbergers only smile and take pride in being thrifty and hard-working. They are content to be different, just as they are content to send their children to schools in Switzerland, in St Gallen or even Zurich, which is much nearer than Innsbruck. After the First World War 80 per cent voted for merger negotiations with Switzerland, but a peace conference decided otherwise, and so they became part of the newly created Austrian Republic. For all of this, the Vorarlbergers are decidedly Austrian. They have the same subtle mixture of liveliness and common sense, solemnity and humour, seriousness and a gaiety which sometimes seems a little forced.

To enjoy the best of the picture-postcard aspects of Vorarlberg, explore the Bregenz Forest, where the villages include the oddly named Egg and Aw (pronounced 'Ow'!), and where women still occasionally wear a stiffly starched dress, the style of which has remained unchanged for at least 600 years; other costume curiosities include a small, golden head-dress worn by unmarried girls during festivals.

An alternative is to join a band of hikers as they set out at dawn from one of the villages of the Montafon Valley; which comprise a scattering of flower-decked chalets and an onion-domed church. On special occasions the girls still wear silk aprons over their heavy full skirts, and put on the fine embroidered lace head-dresses handed down from mother to daughter. The hikers exchange a '*Grüss Gott*' ('God greet you') with the man unloading milk churns, then they are striding along stony, heather-scented paths. From high up on the meadows comes the tinkle of

A typical Austrian landscape – a flowering meadow and a cluster of well-designed homes, at the foot of a range of forested, snow-capped mountains. The Salzkammergut region is honeycombed with lakes and attracts holidaymakers throughout the year. It has been the inspiration of poets, painters and musicians.

cowbells, sometimes carried by the *Föhn*, the dry wind hastening the summer melt that from May fills the trout streams that dash down the mountainsides. As the sun flushes the snowy peaks, you are seized with an exhilarating feeling; it seems as though you have discovered a wilderness unchanged since the dawn of time – only seems, for every tiny footpath is carefully marked. Our hikers do not climb as far as the dazzling glaciers of the Silvretta, but are content to gaze upon them from a distance, seated side by side on a convenient rock. At dusk they will return down the valley, their lungs full of fresh air and faces tanned by sun and wind. Nightfall on the mountains is always an awesome experience, with the peaks still bright-lit by the setting sun when the valleys are plunged into darkness.

Bregenz is the Vorarlberg's capital. Comfortable homes dot its wooded slopes which rise gently from

In the Tyrol, cupboards, chests, beds and chairs were all apt to be painted with floral designs and simple portraits in bright colours. Such peasant furniture is still in demand.

Bodensee (Lake Constance); here live the captains of Austria's textile industry. The businessmen have their artistic side and support a four-week summer music festival, whose floating stage sits on the lake and provides a superb setting for ballet and opera. One of the most breathtaking views in all of Europe is only a six-minute funicular ride from the heart of Bregenz; from the top of Pfänder Mountain, with the Old Town at your feet, you look across the busy modern city to Switzerland on your left and Germany on your right. At such an elevation, it is easier to take in the fact that Bregenz is as close to Paris as it is to Vienna.

A warm family atmosphere

A modern road drives straight through the Arlberg, supervised by a computer to smooth the traffic flow, and burrows for almost nine miles through solid rock to emerge in the Tyrol, a mountain fastness traversed from west to east by the Inn, the river which gives its name to the regional capital, Innsbruck. There are two Tyrols: one full of wild valleys sunk between dizzy cliffs with only the occasional chamois or roe deer to disturb the climber's solitude; the other more wooded and lush, with waterfalls, and meadows speckled with crocuses: a land of farms and chalets and villages with bell towers, red and green churches crowned by gilded onion domes, a land of peasants with pink cheeks and energetic people, determined to keep up traditions.

Because of its distance from Vienna, the Tyrol has always enjoyed some autonomy: as early as the 15th century the people won the right to bear arms and sit

The main room in a typical farmhouse is simple, with dark wood furniture and whitewashed beams and walls. In the old days family life centred on the Stube, a big tiled stove which kept everyone warm through the long winter nights.

The horn player is wearing the floral waistcoat of the Danube, while the two little girls are in the costume of the Wachau Valley, a romantic defile covered with vines and so many fruit trees that in spring the entire valley seems smothered in scented snow.

alongside their overlords in government assemblies. Tyroleans have a reputation for being strong characters, with a certain brutal frankness, as compared with the easy-going Viennese. They fought fiercely against invaders, from the Roman legions to Napoleon's armies, and with the same stout spirit they have withstood the tourists without conceding too much. Their deepest distress is over the loss of the South Tyrol, the rich, red wine country ceded to Italy under the terms of the 1918 peace treaty; cross-border ties remain very strong.

Religion is a highly visible element in Tyrolean life, as it is throughout Austria, which is a bastion of the Catholic faith. The roadsides and mountain paths are full of chapels beckoning the traveller to prayer. Many houses carry religious carvings, pious inscriptions and pictures of saints or the Virgin, and even a tavern may be graced by a crucifix over the door. Churches are filled and remain the focus of country life. Monasteries abound, and many take in paying guests who can enjoy a few days' retreat from everyday life in the most calming and hospitable atmosphere imaginable.

Tyrolean farmhouses are low and squat, usually whitewashed and built into the mountainside; the animals live on the ground floor, and the family on the first floor, snugly insulated by the hay and fodder in the loft. Wherever you go, at home or at an inn, activity centres on the great tiled stoves. The moment you enter an inn, a Tyrolean in leather shorts and thick woollen stockings offers a friendly greeting and a carafe of Magdalener, a light red wine which is reviving rather than intoxicating. On Sundays and feast days, the accordionist sets the fair-haired girls whirling in their pleated skirts, while the boys slap thighs and ankles as they leap up and down, and let out whistles and cries. To complete the clamour, trumpets are sure to be sounding; there are at least 300 brass bands in the Tyrol, and each one is alert to every opportunity to enliven an occasion.

Lech, an attractive village in a valley of the Arlberg Mountains, is also an international resort; many Austrian champions have perfected their skills at its ski schools. The Arlberg is a winter sports paradise, with good snow cover guaranteed on the treeless slopes.

The small church of St Mary at Telfs, on the Inn, ready for Christmas midnight mass. Such churches and chapels, often with rich Rococo interiors, are common throughout the Tyrol.

Bands will often be found giving some 'oomph' to parades of marksmen in their highly coloured costumes and feathered hats. Crack shots are a Tyrol speciality, and so are fine skiers. Modern Alpine ski racing was born at St Anton in 1928, when the English sportsman Arnold Lunn teamed up with local pioneer Hannes Schneider to stage a downhill slalom race to which the best skiers from all over the world were invited. Little St Anton became one of the foremost winter sports centres in the world, and so it has remained. Kitzbühel became the other celebrated Tyrolean resort. Its then mayor, Franz Reisch, brought the first pair of skis from Norway in 1892 and used them in a successful descent from the top of the Kitzbüheler Horn. History does not provide details of the technique used by this heroic pioneer, but it was to be improved upon by another native son, Toni Sailer, seven times world skiing champion. Kitzbühel's facilities have likewise been improved; they include the famous Ski Circus, an arrangement of lifts and runs that provides more than 50 miles of downhill skiing without an inch of uphill clambering by the skier.

Innsbruck, the beautiful city

Innsbruck (Bridge over the Inn) is a beautiful city of red roofs and green domes, and the amazing tomb of Maximilian I, still waiting for the remains of the emperor, who died in 1519. The tomb is the largest of its kind ever built, and it is guarded by statues of 28 of his ancestors; they even include Britain's legendary King Arthur. In fact, the monument was so large that it could not be fitted into the church where the Emperor's body was interred and the Hofkirche had to be built to house it.

The Tyrolean capital is locked between mountain ranges that form a natural crossroads connecting Italy, Germany and Switzerland. The old Baroque town has survived almost intact, and its other sites include the Hofburg Palace and the shimmering Goldenes Dachl (Golden Roof), a mansion with a gilded balcony supposedly built by Duke Friedl 'the Penniless' in an effort to prove to everyone that he was actually quite rich. Lately, Innsbruck has concentrated on sport: the Winter Olympics of 1964 and 1976 were held here. Dominating Innsbruck life is its towering snow backcloth, which is so near and such a lure that young and old will snatch the opportunity of

a lunch-break to crowd aboard the trams which run to the foot of the ski-lifts, only a few minutes away. There is no age limit when it comes to Austrian skiers; they can start at four and carry on well into their seventies.

Winter is not only best for skiing, but also the time for popular festivals; a passion for dressing-up in bright colours is common to all Austrians, and to the Tyroleans in particular. The main round of festivities begins on the Thursday before Lent. The following Monday is considered a good day to get married (though nobody knows why), and a great ball is held on Shrove Tuesday evening, before Lent begins. On the first Sunday in Lent, Branntweinsonntag (Brandy Sunday), the girls give the boys *Faschingskrapfen* (jam-filled doughnuts) and mulled wine.

At Imst, a pretty little town on the Inn, every fifth year sees the Schemenlaufen, or Ghost Race, on the penultimate Sunday in Lent. The 'ghosts', or people wearing masks to make them look like ghosts, run up and down the streets, banging on doors and making as much noise as possible. They are aided in this by the Scheller, carrying pretzels as fertility symbols, and the equally noisy Roller, who hop from foot to foot ringing bells and shaking rattles, while the Spritzer dash water on the ground to make it fertile. Then comes a wrestling match between a bear and a man, which the man (advisedly the bear's trainer) is required to win, since this is a symbolic fight between Winter and Spring. A triumphal dance ensues, with the ghosts shouting themselves hoarse and the others ringing and shaking their bells and rattles as energetically as possible.

Shop and craftsmen's signs have proliferated in Austria since the 17th century, and wrought ironwork is a highly developed art. This sign was made for a locksmith's shop in the Getreidegasse in Salzburg, a street famous for such signs.

Innsbruck, beautiful Baroque capital of the Tyrol, is spectacularly sited at a mountain crossroads, commanding routes to Germany, Italy and Switzerland. The Habsburgs reigned here early in the 15th century, and 300 years later it held out against against French and Bavarian invasion. It has hosted the Winter Olympic Games twice this century.

The Little Golden Roof is an Innsbruck curiosity: a 15th-century house with a fairy-tale balcony covered with 3500 gilded copper tiles. The balcony was originally used by guests of the Imperial court to watch festivities in the square below; now it is used for band concerts.

The Schleicherlaufen (Sly Race) is held every five years in Telfs. Men wearing multi-coloured silk costumes take part in the procession, which originated as a pagan rite intended to drive away the winter and encourage the coming spring.

... and Salzburg, the enchanted city

The perfect cure for such commotion is to proceed quickly to Salzburg, Mozart's birthplace, a riot of Baroque lying beneath the Monchsberg rock, with the 1000-year-old fortress of Hohensalzburg. 'Every square, every street, seems to have been designed like a stage setting', wrote Max Reinhardt, who organised the first Salzburg Festival in 1920, in collaboration with the dramatist Hugo von Hofmannsthal and composer Richard Strauss. The city owes its charm to a happy combination of art and nature, or to what a 1200-year line of prince-archbishops did

to a beautiful setting of river (the Salzach), rocks, forests and distant mountains: they built churches, palaces and noble houses with rare abandon. The most memorable among them was the passionate 16th-century Archbishop Wolf Dietrich, who had 12 children by a beautiful Jewess named Salome Alt; for her, he built the chateau of Mirabell across the Salzach, and because of her, he spent his last five years locked up in the Hohensalzburg. Salzburg owes its continued existence to the good sense of opposing German and American generals who, in 1945, agreed not to turn it into a battlefield; both were later made freemen of the city.

Getreidegasse, a narrow and busy street, is festooned with ancient shop signs. Number 9, once the home of a well-to-do grocer, is where Wolfgang Amadeus, third child of the Mozart family, was born on January 27, 1756. Mozart had been dead for 50 years before Salzburg honoured him with a statue, and it was 130 years before it got round to honouring him with a festival, but now it is an important annual event in the music calendar, running from the last week in July to the end of August and attracting the very best orchestras and artists. At this time the city is packed with visitors, mostly from abroad, and mostly rich, for tickets are very expensive; even so, they are sold out a year in advance.

Salzburg is the capital of the province of the same name. After the Tyrol, even the castles hereabouts are less forbidding, for a lively elegance seems to permeate every aspect of life. Here the best coffee-houses compare with the best in Vienna, and here the Austrian greeting for a lady, 'Küss die

Hand' (I kiss your hand), seems a particularly fitting one. Salzburg's ladies are especially noted for the elegance of their clothes. The young have long abandoned the traditional lederhosen for jeans, but their mothers retain a preference for the green or black loden jacket and skirt, trimmed with velvet. Instead of an overcoat, they wear loden capes which in winter may be lined with beaver or muskrat. Austrian women achieved full legal equality in 1956, with the passing of a law depriving husbands of exaggerated rights over their wives. Where before she could be forbidden from taking a job, today the Austrian wife does not even have to adopt her husband's name; yet social and economic equality are proving harder to achieve. While many women now earn their own living, their salaries are lower, and prejudices in favour of the traditional woman's role as housewife are very much alive.

Actors waiting to make their entrance during a performance of Hofmannsthal's 'Jedermann' (Everyman), staged in front of the 17th-century cathedral during the annual Salzburg Festival. The effect of the surroundings is stunning, particularly when Death makes his appearance. The Festival was conceived in 1920 as a tribute to Mozart, and attracts the world's greatest conductors, musicians and singers.

The salt mines

Salz in German means 'salt'. It was the salt mines that created the wealth of the province and of the city, for salt was such a precious commodity that it was a government monopoly. The largest mines were above the town of Hallein, home of Franz-Xaver Gruber, composer of the Christmas carol, *Stille Nacht, Heilige Nacht* (*Silent night, Holy night*). To visit a mine, you put on white overalls and ride a toboggan down to a subterranean world of salt lakes, plied by flat-bottomed boats. The visit includes a hair-raising ride in a small truck along seemingly endless salt corridors which reveals a fascinating and surprising underground world of sparkle and glitter.

The Salzkammergut, the salt-bearing region, begins to the east of Salzburg, but most of it lies under the *Land* of Upper Austria. This is a province of forest, rugged mountain and limpid lakes looking

The narrow, usually crowded Getreidegasse (Grain Street) is the main thoroughfare of old Salzburg. Mozart was born at No 9. Most of the houses date from the 16th and 17th centuries, and there are many shops, boutiques and cafés, all with intricate wrought-iron signs.

Decorations in trompe-l'oeil (Luftlmalerei) are a feature of many houses in the Tyrol and the Salzkammergut. The craft was handed down from father to son, and enlivened many otherwise dull façades. This one now graces a cake and sweet shop.

The Grundlsee in the Salzkammergut offers perfect peace amid spectacular scenery. In spite of the many visitors who flock to their country, the Austrians are ardent ecologists who have always known how to conserve their natural resources, while providing the best in hospitality.

like huge eyes 'edged with reeds like long emerald lashes', or so the French poet Mallarmé has it. These lakes have inspired many musicians. St Wolfgang was the setting for the popular operetta *White Horse Inn* (the inn still functions as a commercial operation), while Wagner composed *Tristan and Isolde* on the shores of the Traunsee, a lake with steep cliffs rising sheer from the water. Hallstatt Lake is famous for a different reason: archaeological research along its shores has uncovered several Iron Age settlements, as well as the body of a prehistoric miner perfectly preserved by the salt for thousands of years.

At Hallstatt, squeezed tightly between the lake and a mountain, the salt mines are still being worked.

The town is on such a steep slope that the houses have hanging gardens and are tiered one above the other, while people living on the shore line use boats to get about; a road into Hallstatt was not built until 1890. A summer playground today, the Salz-kammergut (it means Estate of the Salt Chamber) was once so jealously guarded that no one was allowed in or out, for fear of salt smugglers. It was not until the 19th century that it was opened up after the young Emperor Franz Joseph began to spend his summers there, and the aristocracy flocked in.

The Danube may be eternally blue in the popular imagination, but it varies from milky to murky when in spate, and usually it is a muddy brown as it

glides majestically through Upper and Lower Austria, through regions of hills and vineyards, past picturesque terraced villages and occasionally striking architecture, like Melk Abbey, best viewed on its rocky spur in the golden light of sunset. Rising in the Black Forest, and charged by Alpine tributaries, the Danube is fully navigable throughout Austria, and this is important for several industrial centres. After Melk the river enters the valley of the Wachau, where the Babenbergs, the first Austrian dynasty, built their stronghold at the end of the 10th century. This is great wine-growing country, where a pine branch hung outside an inn indicates that the owner makes his own wine. Some of the wines have extraordinary names, like Himmelstiege (Leap to Heaven), Katzensprung (Cat's Leap) and Flohhaxn (Flea's Foot). Ever since the Romans used the Danube as a barrier against the barbarians, this corridor between eastern and western Europe has been a prime target of all conquerors, and there are well over 500 castles in Lower Austria to testify to this.

The names Upper and Lower Austria denote their relative positions along the course of the Danube; they are the original territories of the Archduchy of Austria from which the empire sprang. The people who live in the north, between the river and the Czech frontier, are known as hard-working, if somewhat dour. The Iron Curtain severed the region's intimate links with Bohemia, but many refugees from there settled here, bringing with them special skills in glass- and crystal-making. Linz, the capital of Upper Austria, is where the old salt route reached the Danube. This ancient city has suffered from industrialisation; its streets are garish with neon, and its old houses, dwarfed by steel and chemical factories, create a feeling of melancholy.

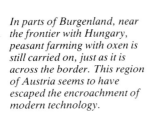

In parts of Burgenland, near the frontier with Hungary, peasant farming with oxen is still carried on, just as it is across the border. This region of Austria seems to have escaped the encroachment of modern technology.

Two happy provinces

The sadness fades as you travel south towards Styria and Carinthia. Styria, often called 'the green heart of Austria', is a land of high valleys and the densest forests in Austria. It is also rich in minerals. The Erzberg (Ore Mountain) is an enormous stepped pyramid where the iron is extracted by open-cast mining. It was the major source of the Austrian Empire's industrial power. According to legend, a gnome gave the people a choice between mining gold for 20 months, silver for 20 years, or iron for ever; the people wisely chose the last.

In the isolated farms of the high Styrian valleys, a patriarchal way of life survives almost intact. Households are headed by the Master (Herr) and this title, which also means 'lord', is strictly observed. Meals are taken in the *Stube*, the big living-room, in the *Herrgottswinkel* (the Lord God's Corner), so called because the crucifix is hung in the angle above the table. The lord of the house presides, and his Frau (wife) does the cooking, helped by a servant. Everyone eats together. Even a few years ago, such a household would consist of 10 to 15 people. Their herd, going up to the alpine meadows in summer, usually consists of 40 to 50 cows, with perhaps a few goats, in the care of a *Sennerin* (cowgirl) and a *Melker* (milker). Once a week, such basic provisions

The Riesenrad, *the Big Wheel in Vienna, was memorably featured in the Carol Reed film* The Third Man. *A ride on the Big Wheel is part of any Sunday outing to the Prater, a huge wooded park that was an Imperial hunting forest and is now a pleasure ground. There were sister wheels in London and Paris, but they disappeared long ago.*

as bread, flour, salt, sugar, lard and paraffin are carried up to their mountain hut.

Graz, capital of Styria and the second largest city in Austria, is no longer the 'Pensionopolis' of the days of the monarchy, when retired civil servants and officers came here to end their days. Nor is it the strongest fortress in Christendom, as it was in the 15th century when it commanded the 'Western Wall' against Turkish invasion. Now a busy modern city, it has retained charming old neighbourhoods with arcaded houses, often richly decorated. Its many cafés are a rendezvous for artists, writers and intellectuals. Here, as in other parts of Austria, strangers are often addressed as 'Herr Doktor', a form of exaggerated politeness and also a reflection of the Austrians' love of titles. Some people claim, however, that the custom continues simply to make life easier. By calling everyone 'Herr Doktor' you do not have to remember their name.

The more curious attractions of Graz include the 17th-century Zeughaus (arsenal), which holds a

unique collection of weapons and armour from the Middle Ages; there are 30,000 pieces in all, mostly fashioned from Styrian iron and tested in battle against the Turks, and all arranged in perfect order, ready for the knights' return. Not far from Graz is the famous Piber stud, where the magnificent Lippizaner stallions are raised and trained to perform at the Spanish Riding School in Vienna. Their lineage can be traced back to 1580, when the stud (then situated near Trieste) was set up with stallions from Arabia and mares from Spain. Almost black when they are born, they turn smoky grey as they grow older and by the age of eight are snow-white. They need an intensive two-year schooling before they are ready for the exacting public performances.

The Viennese like to take their holidays in Carinthia, the southernmost province, where the publicity brochures would have you believe that there is a certainty of 2000 hours' sunshine every year. This 'Austrian Riviera' boasts of 198 lakes and countless castles. Here is the highest peak in Austria, the

majestic Grossglockner (nearly 12,500 feet). The first to climb it, in July 1800, was the local prince-bishop of Gurk, who took with him four young men equipped with thick ropes and cumbersome wooden ladders, for there were no ice-axes or crampons in those days. The courage required was extraordinary and decades later the early mountaineer H. D. Inglis

was relieved when a providential storm prevented him from what he called the 'pure folly' of embarking on the same ascent 'above the line of eternal frost'. Nowadays, an excellent mountain road provides superb panoramas at every turn.

For more than a thousand years, Slovene and German have lived side by side within Carinthia's

After riding the Big Wheel, the dodgems and the roundabouts, this teenager is getting her teeth into another of the delights of the Prater. This vast fairground has many restaurants.

Demel, Vienna's best-known pastry shop, achieved fame as caterer to the Habsburg court. Its uniformed waitresses invite customers to savour an incomparable choice of superb delicacies, all hand-made to traditional recipes.

girdle of mountains, fighting each other occasionally, but more often living in harmony. After the tragic period of the Nazi domination, and the forced Germanisation that went with it, the small Slovene minority have their own schools again, and a university where the teaching is in their own tongue. However, the dominant language is German, which the young people must learn if they want to work anywhere outside their native valley.

Carinthia is agricultural and intensely Catholic: there are no fewer than 243 sanctuaries dedicated to the Virgin Mary, while several chapels honour local saints unknown elsewhere. At Friesach, still a town of moats and ramparts to guard the old route from Vienna to Venice, something akin to a medieval version of the Olympics used to take place. In May 1224, 600 knights participated in one tournament; they included the 'May Knight' Ulrich von Liechtenstein, a distinguished troubadour who caused a stir by turning out in an all-green kit and breaking 53 lances on his opponents.

The Viennese sea

The Viennese are fond of poking fun at the people of Burgenland; their reputation as bumpkins is hardly deserved, though it is true that theirs is a world apart. Here begins the great Hungarian plain. Tourists become rarer, hotels less frequent and the people much less sophisticated, and even though it is only a short bus ride from Vienna, the province seems to have retreated behind the crenellated crests of the 'stone curtain' that saved it from Turk and Mongol. The villages of low, thatched cottages have an old-world feel to them – geese waddling noisily down to the pond, bunches of maize drying under the eaves, a man in high boots watering his horse at a well. Around each village stretches the plain, bleak and melancholy landscape, as far as the eye can see.

It is a strange land, and nothing about it is stranger than the Neusiedler See, sometimes the largest lake in Austria. This sheet of water is so shallow (seven feet at its deepest) that it occasionally disappears into the ground. Depending upon atmospheric pressure and wind direction, it expands southwards, where there is nothing to contain it, or sloshes from side to side, leaving stretches of the opposite shore quite dry. It is fed by one river, the Wulka, which contributes only a quarter of the water lost to evaporation; nobody is certain where the rest comes from. Logically the lake should have disappeared long ago, and during a long dry spell it will do so and cause bitter disputes over the ownership of the exposed land, until one fine day it is back again. That is what happened in 1868–72. In summer, the fickle lake becomes the 'Viennese Sea' where trippers from the capital can swim, sail or row. Its reed-covered shores are a paradise for birds and bird-watchers; more than 270 species have been recorded.

Eisenstadt, the capital of the Burgenland, exemplifies the calm, soft, somewhat enigmatic attitude of the province. The imposing castle of the princely Esterhazy family, and the much more modest house once occupied by Joseph Haydn, the family composer, escaped the destruction of the last war, but only a museum recalls that here lived one of the largest and oldest-established Jewish communities in Austria. A few Jews managed to escape the Nazis and establish new homes overseas; some joined earlier emigrant groups, including a large contingent which made its way to America early this century. This explains why Burgenland has unexpected numbers of dollar millionaires – and why one little settlement on the Hungarian border is called Chicago.

The capital of nostalgia

Vienna, city of dreams and waltzes, of grandeur and the Habsburgs, of *The Third Man*, of sadness and ruins, is today rebuilt, beautiful, and seems contented. On the surface, at least, it is, for this capital that once ruled half of Europe is still capital of an empire of nostalgia. Everything that has happened since the abdication of the Emperor in 1918 seems to have been the actions of smaller people.

In the Hofburg, the majestic palace now turned into the museum of a vanished empire, Franz Joseph's rooms have been kept as he knew them, with the small iron bed, the toilet table and the tiny jug and basin he used for washing. Nearby are the apartments of the Empress Elizabeth, where she heard of the death of her son Rudolph. He had shot

The Naglergasse, a narrow street in the heart of one of the oldest districts in Vienna, is a pedestrian mall of small, old-fashioned shops. This little bakery supplies diabetics with specially made cakes.

himself and one of his mistresses, Baroness Marie Versera, at his hunting lodge at Mayerling on the morning of January 31, 1889. In the dining room, the table is laid ready for the entire Imperial family. Near the Hofburg, in the crypt of the chapel of the Capuchins, lie the remains of 138 members of the Habsburg dynasty, with a last empty place destined to remain that way.

'Asia begins at the gates of Vienna,' said Count Metternich, the architect of European diplomacy after Waterloo and an Austrian by adoption. This city at the centre of Europe has had gates open in all directions for so long that the complex Viennese character ('grumpy and cranky, arrogant and melancholy,' according to its own tourist board) is a subject in itself. To be a 'true' Viennese, you need to have a great-grandfather from Moravia, a grandmother from Budapest, a Croatian uncle and a cousin living in Trieste – which explains some of the mysteries of

Old Vienna lives on, so long as there are violinists like these contented veterans to play the music of the waltz kings, the Strausses, father and son.

the telephone directory.

How does the true Viennese live? Most likely he will be a civil servant, for bureaucracy still flourishes in Austria. He will rise early, since banks and most businesses open at 8 am, and make for a café whenever offices empty at 5 pm. Bags of coffee beans were left by the Turks in their flight of 1683, and the Viennese acquired a taste for it. On Saturday everything shuts at noon, and on Sunday only the cafés are open, and are as busy as ever. In the old cafés in the heart of the city the waiters do not object to your spending half the morning in front of an empty cup of coffee, while you read newspapers that are provided free of charge. Even if you try to place an order, they

Balls are still an important feature of Viennese life, and are particularly plentiful during the carnival season. This is the annual Concordia Ball, which attracts writers, journalists and diplomats; it is privileged to use the great ballroom of the City Hall, which rarely opens its neo-Gothic interior to visitors.

are past masters in the art of ignoring you, but when you do catch their eye, you are liable to be deferentially addressed with one of the many titles so sweet to Austrian ears – such as 'Herr Doktor' – even though such terms were officially discarded with the passing of the old empire. Such places are club, pub, bistro and home-away-from-home for the Viennese, safe harbours of a lifestyle rescued from the shattered past. If coffee (and it comes in a dozen varieties) is not enough, explore beneath the streets to find some ancient cellar where a glass of white wine is a perfect complement to the quartet playing Viennese music. Then look around and consider how successfully the Viennese have turned time around, and relaxed the pace of living.

The café of the Hotel Sacher is always full: here elegant ladies meet between 5 and 6 pm to exchange gossip and display their finery, and to enjoy a *Wiener Eiskaffee* (black coffee with ice cream) and a slice of *Sachertorte*, the renowned chocolate cake created by the Hotel's founder, Madame Sacher. Such small items will not interfere with the ladies' appetites for dinner, though often it will be a cold meal: meats and various sausages, salads, cheese, and perhaps stewed or fresh fruit. Breakfast usually consists of coffee with milk, a boiled egg, hot rolls and croissants, assorted jams, butter and honey. This may be bolstered by *Gabelfrühstück* (hot goulash and sausages) at around 11 am. Lunch is usually soup, followed by a big main dish, *Wienerschnitzel* (veal fried in egg and breadcrumbs) with potato salad, or half a chicken perhaps, then a dessert of Viennese pastry, rich and luscious and sunk in *Schlagobers*, their beloved whipped cream. On Sundays in summer, the Viennese often go to a *Heurigen*, a bar in the suburbs of Grinzing or Sievering, where young wine is the speciality.

Dancing to the Viennese tune

Vienna sprawls over 23 districts that together make up one of the nine provinces of the republic. Of its many parks and gardens, the best known are those of the palace of Schönbrunn (where Marie Antoinette grew up) and the Belvedere. There is also the Prater, an elegant rendezvous in the hey-day of the Viennese waltz, and now a popular pleasure park, with the Big Wheel as its main attraction. The Wheel takes 20 minutes to complete one revolution, which is time enough to enjoy the views of the city and its green copper roofs, its towers and domes. The centre-piece of the old city is the cathedral of St Stephan, with its 450-foot steeple outmatching that of Salisbury Cathedral by a clear 46 feet. Battered by 17th-century Turks and 20th-century Russians and Germans, it has been completely restored, with every Austrian province contributing to the cost. The Ring, a wide, curving succession of boulevards, garlands the old city with rather pompous 19th-century buildings, from neo-Grecian (the Parliament building) to neo-Gothic (the city hall). A newcomer

is the futuristic United Nations building, part of an effort to make Vienna, after New York and Geneva, a third capital of this world body.

Amid this architectural confectionery the Danube is rather hard to find. Surely it cannot be that ugly grey snake coiling around the Old Quarter? Not exactly, for that is the 'Canal', an arm of the river, whose main stream lies out beyond the Prater. But Blue Danube it is, and will remain, for waltz king Johann Strauss deemed it to be so, and his creations are ingrained in Vienna's soul. Mozart, Schubert, Beethoven, Haydn, the Strausses, Mahler, Bruckner, Lehar and Brahms all brought their talents here, and a single tram ride from the city centre will take you past the house where Mozart wrote his last three symphonies (in six weeks!) and the street where Beethoven died, the house where Schubert was born

Lippiza, near Trieste, was home of the Lippizaner horses for more than 300 years. They originally came from Spain and were used to train the sons of the nobility – hence the name of the 'Spanish Riding School'.

and another where Beethoven worked, and at the end of the tram track, on the edge of the Vienna Woods, you can have a drink in a tavern where Beethoven stayed, and follow the path he took before writing the *Pastoral Symphony*.

The Opera House, destroyed in 1945 and lovingly rebuilt, is not merely world-famous, but is a major focus of Viennese life. Families hold season tickets inherited down several generations. A performance here is as much ritual as entertainment, and audience participation is intense: so much so that the Staatsoper (Vienna State Opera) audiences, in particular the regulars of the Stehplätze (standing area), with their high-pitched Viennese intonations, are considered the most volatile in all of Europe by the celebrities who nevertheless are eager to appear before them. The post of Opera Director carries the same sort of status as the country's president, and the incumbent is subject to much greater and more constant public scrutiny. Yet the Viennese are not burdened by musical snobbery, even if they are bigoted against heroes other than their own, and operettas like *The Merry Widow*, *The Gypsy Baron* and *Die Fledermaus* are performed and appreciated with the same sense of pride as the waltzes of the Strauss family are still danced.

The Vienna Philharmonic, a national treasure as much as an orchestra, does double duty in playing for the State Opera, and giving its own regular performances on Sundays. On New Year's Day, when it plays only the works of the Strauss family, it seems as though all of Vienna attends.

At first light, the Lippizaners go out to exercise in the Prater or the Vienna Woods; later will come performances in the Riding School of the Hofburg. There is still no written manual, and the skills continue to be passed down from generation to generation by example.

Gazetteer

France

The largest country in western Europe, France is increasingly one of the most prosperous as it moves to integrate more closely with its neighbours. However, a great deal of its history is characterised by attempts to dominate these surrounding countries, adventures that frequently had a destabilising effect on the French state.

Much of the evidence of the arrival of modern man in Europe is provided by the caves of south-west France, where hunter-gatherers settled about 35,000 years ago, painting the images of their quarry on the cave walls. Farming and stone tool-making technology spread to the region from the western Mediterranean about 4000 BC, encouraging settlers to move to the plains where farming could flourish. By 2000 BC well-organised communities were living in Brittany where they raised the massive stone

monuments known as megaliths, over 1000 of which remain on the Breton coast at Carnac to this day.

Between 1500 and 1000 BC the Celts took control of much of Europe; the Romans called these tribes Gauls. As the power of Rome grew, so did the friction between them and their northern neighbours. However, it was not until Julius Caesar led his legions against a poorly organised federation of Celtic tribes between 58 and 50 BC that much territory north of the Alps came under Roman control.

Roman engineers built the network of paved roads, bridges and towns that linked these newly conquered lands, and Latin became the local language. However, as Rome's power faded in the 5th century AD, fierce Germanic tribes such as the Alemanni and the Franks attacked the Romanised Gauls and, after the Huns sacked Rome in 455, the old order collapsed.

Tribes from the north-east moved in to fill the power

vacuum, each with their own language. The Visigoths took over territory close to the Mediterranean and the Atlantic coast as far north as modern Bordeaux. The Burgundians controlled most of the Rhône Valley, while the Franks dominated the north. From the end of the 5th century to the beginning of the 8th the Franks tried to conquer their neighbours but they were handicapped by their custom of dividing a king's territory equally amongst his sons on his death.

During the 7th century Europe was threatened by the rising tide of Islam. Arab power swept rapidly along the coast of North Africa, and then penetrated Spain and France as far north as the Rhône Valley. Only when the Arabs were confronted by the Franks led by Charles Martel at the battle of Poitiers in 732 were they defeated. When Martel's grandson Charlemagne became the king of the Franks in 768 he enlarged his domain, and his empire eventually extended from the Baltic in the north as far south as Corsica. However, the old rules of royal inheritance were revived and soon the Frankish Empire was dismembered.

In the 9th and 10th centuries, the Vikings erupted from their base in Scandinavia. In 911 the Frankish king Charles the Simple recognised their control of Normandy. Under William the Conqueror the Norman-Vikings over-ran England and in the process became much more powerful than their nominal king who only maintained firm control of the Ile-de-France region that surrounds modern Paris.

For much of the next 400 years, the control of central and northern France became a tug of war between these two groups. The struggle for power was only resolved in 1453 when the English were finally ejected from all but the tiny fragment of France surrounding Calais.

However, the years of conflict had placed a great deal of power in the hands of the French commanders, the princes of regions such as Picardy and Burgundy that Paris could barely control. During the second half of the 15th century French kings were preoccupied with asserting their authority over these territories, frequently fighting full-scale wars to do so.

As the nation's wealth increased, merchant families rose to prominence and bought land to reinforce their political power. French society was thrown into even greater ferment by the rapid growth of the Protestant faith in France and its persecution by Francis I during the first half of the 16th century.

In 1559 the French king was killed in a jousting match. When his son became ill and died just a year later France, without a direct heir to the throne, was plunged into a civil war that lasted 30 years as two families, the Guises and the Bourbons, fought for supremacy. Religious rivalry played its part as the Guise family were the leaders of the French Catholics while the Bourbons were Protestants. The crisis came to a head in 1586 when Henry of Navarre, a Protestant and a member of the Bourbon family, became the legitimate heir to the throne. His solution was to become a Catholic, assume the crown and destroy his enemies. To end the religious feuding he issued the Edict of Nantes in 1598 which allowed his Protestant subjects freedom of worship.

Henry was a shrewd monarch who surrounded himself with able ministers but his assassination in 1610 threw the French state back into turmoil. His son, Louis XIII, was only nine years old at the time and was soon caught up in the factions that intrigued for power at court. Eventually, in 1624, the King's mother introduced Cardinal Richelieu to the Council of State as chief minister, and an alliance between the King and cardinal was formed that destroyed the power of the French aristocracy for a generation. Unfortunately, Richelieu and Louis both died in 1643 when the heir to the throne was only four years old. Again, France was thrown into chaos that did not end until the young King, Louis XIV, assumed the reins of power in 1661.

The 50 years that followed are among the most splendid in French history. Louis was renowned throughout Europe as the Sun King because of the magnificence of his court. However, the extravagance was not just self-indulgence on the King's part. By forcing his courtiers to adopt his lavish style he put them under considerable financial pressure that made it difficult for them to build up large armies of retainers that might threaten the monarchy.

Louis' foreign policy was not so well thought out and resulted in long and expensive wars that brought France close to bankruptcy. He also made a serious blunder in revoking the protection given to French Protestants by the Edict of Nantes. Many fled abroad, taking with them industrial skills that France could ill afford to lose.

As the 18th century opened, the French government was in a difficult position. Wars had drained France's financial resources and the country's industrial base had been weakened; a period of stability was needed in which to restore the economy. Yet France became drawn into conflict after conflict, and to pay for these hostilities citizens who had previously been exempt had to be taxed. The aristocracy and the clergy had privileges and tax exemptions denied to the rising and resentful middle classes.

By 1789 the government had little alternative but to call the first meeting for 175 years of the Estates General, which was roughly equivalent to the British parliament. However, while the King wanted an increase in taxation, the representatives wished to air their grievances. This opportunity to publicise their resentment only encouraged the people to become more vocal in their protests and it was not long before riots broke out in towns and cities throughout France.

The Estates General was divided into three parts – the first representing the aristocracy, the second representing the clergy and the Third Estate representing the rest of the country. Although its members were drawn solely from the wealthy middle class, the Third Estate became more and more radical as the summer of 1789 wore on. On June 17 it renamed itself the National Assembly and began making decisions on its own. At first the King opposed this but the Assembly dug in its heels. After the King appeared to concede he secretly mobilised his troops, which caused the Parisian people to lose faith in him and form their own militia. On July 14 they stormed the old royal fortress of the Bastille in the east of Paris, then being used as a prison.

Fearing reprisals by the aristocracy, French peasants throughout the country armed themselves. To regain control, the Assembly proposed the abolition of the feudal rights of the aristocracy in return for compensation, but the peasants would be appeased by nothing less than complete freedom and over the next three years armed rebellions broke out all over France.

In Paris the Assembly attempted a series of consitutional reforms but when the King attempted to flee the country on June 20, 1791, further compromise seemed impossible. In August other European monarchs declared that they would intervene on his behalf. France retaliated by declaring war on Austria in April 1792. However, the combined armies of Prussia and Austria swept the French aside. Now the Assembly had little alternative but to arm the people. On August 10 a popular insurrection overthrew the constitution and declared a republic based on universal suffrage. The Assembly was replaced by a National Convention.

The Convention first met on September 20, 1792, the day that the new Revolutionary Army defeated the invading armies north of Paris. Throughout the autumn rival factions contested the leadership of the Convention, a struggle that was won by the radicals. Their victory led to the trial and execution of the King.

This collapse of the status quo in time of war led to a witch-hunt for other enemies of the new order and an orgy of blood-letting ensued in which the guillotine reigned supreme. Even the leaders of the radicals were consumed by the frenzy of vengeance and only the execution in July 1794 of Robespierre, the most uncompromising of the Convention's leaders, burst the bloody bubble.

The committees of the Convention were replaced by five Directors who tried to distract the nation from its unresolved internal conflicts by an enterprising foreign policy. It was in the campaigns in Italy against the Austrian army that Napoleon Bonaparte first came to public notice, and when he returned from the 1799 Egyptian campaign he was greeted everywhere as a hero. Parisian political factions saw him as a useful figurehead and he was appointed the first among the three consuls who would run France.

However, it was soon clear that such a position would not be enough to satisfy Napoleon's ambitions. By mixing magnanimous gestures to the aristocrats who had fled abroad with severe measures against royalist brigands who were terrorising parts of the country, he steered a middle course that secured his hold on France. He turned a failed assassination plot against him by the royalists in December 1800 to his advantage by blaming the radical left and having many of their leaders deported. By 1802 he was in a strong enough position to have himself confirmed as First Consul for life in a nationwide plebiscite. In 1804 he had himself proclaimed Emperor and staged a coronation in which he was to be crowned by the Pope. But at the last moment he took the crown and placed it on his own head, underlining where the power really lay. As with the Sun King, it was Napoleon's foreign adventures that finally brought him low, despite years of victories. When his source of power, the Grand Army, was destroyed in the retreat from Moscow in 1812, he was at the mercy of the foreign powers ranged against him, primarily Britain and Prussia. After he abdicated in 1814 he was banished to the island of Elba. Despite his escape and final flourish of the following year, his humiliation at Waterloo spelled the end and exile in St Helena.

When the victorious powers reluctantly restored the Bourbon family to the French throne the royalists took their opportunity to exact revenge and tried to restore the France they had known before the revolution. By 1830 the French people were impatient of censorship and an electoral system that allowed fewer than 100,000 citizens to vote where more than 3 million had participated in the plebiscites under Napoleon. After an election in July 1830 in which his ministers were humiliated, the King imposed even more stringent restrictions on the people and then went off on holiday. Faced with such complacency, the people of Paris began erecting barricades across the streets of the capital. Within four days Louis-Phillippe, the Duke of Orléans, was being cheered as the people's choice to replace the King. By August 9 the French parliament had confirmed the acclamation of the street and named him king.

The following 18 years were characterised by uneventful constitutional monarchy, and yet just a few days of crisis mismanagement in February 1848 were enough to end the line of the French monarchy forever. As political meetings were banned, the opposition began organising political banquets. But even these intimidated the government and they tried to stop a banquet arranged for February 22. Students and workers took to the streets and a protest turned into a riot. On the following evening the crowd clashed with an army unit which shot 40 people dead. By the next morning an angry mob was threatening the King's palace and he was so frightened that he abdicated.

A republic was proclaimed in which the government would be elected by universal suffrage. But when elections were held in April the result was a triumph for the conservatives. In the presidential election at the end of the year Napoleon's nephew, Louis-Napoleon, won by a landslide. For two years the President played a cautious game but when it became clear that the assembly would not help him to pay off his debts he staged a coup d'état. At the end of 1852 he had himself proclaimed Emperor.

The years that followed were prosperous ones and the opportunity was taken to rebuild Paris, driving broad, elegant boulevards through the old districts. But like so many French leaders before him, the Emperor could not resist the foreign adventures that eventually brought him down. In 1870 he allowed himself to be provoked into declaring war on Prussia. The result was a humiliating defeat that ushered in the Third Republic.

The new government's first task was to negotiate peace with the Germans. But Paris refused to accept the agreement and unilaterally declared its independence. When the French government sent in troops to crush the rebellion the resulting bloodbath cost 20,000 lives.

During the following decades France joined in the European scramble for territory in Africa and Asia and the country grew more aware that it was being increasingly overshadowed by the growth of German industrial and political power. To try to protect itself, France became involved in a series of alliances, first with Russia and then with Britain. Germany responded by allying itself with the Austro-Hungarian Empire and Italy. In 1914 rivalry between the weakest governments on both sides, Russia and Austro-Hungary, dragged their partners into a four-year conflict, the Great War, with only Italy remaining aloof at first. France lost over 2 million men – 10 per cent of its workforce – before the armistice was declared in 1918.

The next 20 years were an indecisive period for France in which the country lacked clear political direction. Still intimidated by Germany, it built along its eastern border the massive fortifications known as the Maginot Line. But when war came the German army merely went round the end of the still-incomplete line and routed the French in little more than ten days. Only a previously obscure tank commander, Charles de Gaulle, refused to accept defeat and established a government in exile in London.

One of the most active guerrilla groups that resisted the German forces of occupation was led by the Communist Party. However, after the country's liberation by Anglo-American troops the Communists were systematically excluded from the French government, which was headed by de Gaulle. After he resigned in 1946 the country was run by a string of leaders, many of whom lasted no more than a matter of weeks.

However, France was training a generation of technocrats who began to improve the running of French business, the civil service and nationalised industries towards the end of the 1950s. This improvement coincided with the return of de Gaulle in 1958 as the country's leader and the signing of the Treaty of Rome the previous year, which formed the basis of the European Community. De Gaulle extricated France from a bloody war of decolonisation in Algeria and turned the country towards an increasingly prosperous future in which guaranteed farm prices and more competitive industries gave France the confidence to participate actively in the further European integration that will occur in the 1990s.

FRANCE AT A GLANCE

Area 212,740 square miles

Population 56,160,000

Capital Paris

Government Presidential-parliamentary republic

Currency Franc = 100 centimes

Languages French; some Basque, Breton, Catalan, Corsican, Provençal

Religion Christian (mainly Roman Catholic)

Climate Temperate, with hot, dry summers on the Mediterranean coast. Average temperature in Paris ranges from 1–6°C (34–43°F) in January to 14–25°C (57–77°F) in July

Main primary products Cattle, sheep, pigs, poultry, sugar beet, wheat, barley, maize, oats, potatoes, wine, fruit and vegetables; timber; fish; iron ore, bauxite, coal, uranium, salt, oil and natural gas, potash

Major industries Iron and steel, engineering, chemicals, textiles, electrical goods, cars, aircraft, cement, aluminium, agriculture, perfume, forestry, fishing, food processing, oil and gas refining

Main exports Cars, chemicals, iron and steel, textiles, leather goods, electrical equipment, wine, cereals, processed foods, petroleum products, clothing

Annual income per head (US$) 13,020

Population growth (per thous/yr) 4.0

Life expectancy (yrs) Male 72 Female 80

Belgium and Luxembourg

These two countries lie at the crossroads of Europe and occupy a key strategic position on the continent. It is not surprising, therefore, that neither was allowed to enjoy its independence until the 19th century.

Charlemagne's empire was centred on eastern Belgium and the country benefited greatly from his rule. He promoted the establishment of wool manufacturing, which was to be the source of the country's wealth for centuries. After the dismemberment of the Frankish Empire the region broke up into many small principalities and its prosperity diminished for a time, but by AD 1000 it had become one of the richest areas in Europe.

After the turmoil of the early stages of the 100 Years' War between Britain and France, the Duchy of Burgundy annexed the area. Thus, when the last duke died in battle and his daughter Mary married into the Habsburg family in 1477, the country fell into the hands of the Austrian dynasty. After the Spanish branch of the Habsburgs had taken control of the Netherlands and the Dutch had won their freedom in the late 17th century, what was now known as the Spanish Netherlands became a battleground between France and Spain. From 1700 to 1713 it was controlled by France. Then it passed into the hands of Austria. After a brief period of independence during the 1790s, Belgium was again over-run by the French. Only in 1830 did the country finally gain control of its own destiny. Despite its neutrality, its strategic importance was so great that it was the scene of major battles in both world wars. It is little wonder that Brussels, the country's capital, is so enthusiastic about the stability promised by European integration.

The tiny Duchy of Luxembourg did not achieve independence until 1867, having been batted around between Burgundy, the Habsburgs, France and the Netherlands in much the same way as Belgium. Although the Duchy is small, it sits astride a major deposit of iron ore which has made it one of Europe's leading steel producers. It has also used its independence to create laws favourable to the international banking community, which has responded by making the capital an important financial centre.

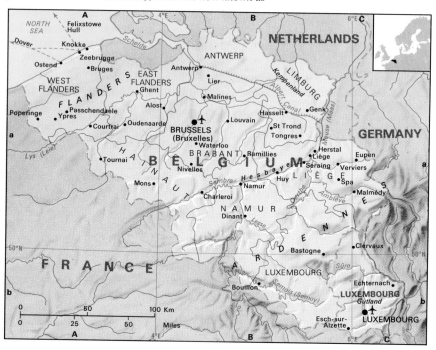

The Netherlands

The Netherlands is a country carved from the sea. For hundreds of years the Dutch have striven to reclaim shallow coastal land, driven on by the desire to give an expanding population a more secure life.

The two ancient German tribes that history first records as migrating to the Rhine delta at the end of the 1st century BC, the Batavians and the Friesians, are still remembered in the names of Dutch provinces. However, the first settlers of the area were the Celts whose many tombs have been excavated in the north-east of the country.

The Romans used the Rhine as a natural border to their empire so only the southern parts of the Netherlands came under their direct control, although their influence undoubtedly reached the tribes to the north of the river. When the legions retreated during the 5th century AD the area came under the control of the Franks. After their empire was dismembered under the rules of royal inheritance during the 9th century, much of the Netherlands fragmented into small, competing feudal states. One of the largest was that ruled by the Count of Holland.

During the Middle Ages a number of Dutch towns took control of their own affairs. The increasingly prosperous merchants of towns such as Utrecht and Dordrecht came to control local finances and elected offices. Beneath them, and frequently in opposition to them, were the local tradesmen and skilled artisans who were trying to develop professional associations to protect their livelihoods and status. During the 13th century the Counts of Holland encouraged this spirit of independence and the towns were given charters with extensive rights.

In the second half of the 14th century the Burgundians tried to extend their power into the area. In 1369 Philip of Burgundy married the daughter of the Count of Flanders, and when his father-in-law died in 1384 the Duchy gained control of much of modern Belgium and parts of the Netherlands. As time passed the Burgundians sought to extend their territories, hoping to establish their own kingdom between the Franks to the south and the Germanic

principalities to the north. However, the death of Charles the Bold in 1477 with only a daughter, Mary, to inherit the Duchy meant that Burgundy fell into the hands of the French king while her lands in the Low Countries passed to Mary's husband, a member of the Habsburg family that ruled Austria. When her son Charles inherited the Spanish crown in 1504, the Netherlands became a pawn in a game aimed at European domination.

Charles had been born and brought up in the Netherlands and sympathised with the culture and traditions of the region. The independence of the towns had created a tradition of tolerance that allowed independent religious sects to develop unmolested. Although Charles was a loyal Catholic he refused to interfere when Calvinism and other forms of the Protestant faith flourished among the Dutch during the first half of the 16th century. However, when his son Philip took over the running of the Habsburg territory in the Low Countries in 1555 he had no scruples about bringing the population to heel. In collusion with the Pope he had three new archbishops and fifteen bishops appointed.

Resistance to Philip, who was now King, and the Catholic Church intensified over the next ten years and in 1566 Protestant fanatics began vandalising Catholic churches. The flames of discontent were fanned by epidemics, poor harvests, floods and rampant inflation. Philip's response was to impose one of his generals, the Duke of Alba, as the new governor.

The Duke set about suppressing sedition with the tools of the Spanish Inquisition – torture, arbitrary arrest, heavy prison sentences and widespread executions – in a country which had a tradition of tolerance. The consequence was guerrilla warfare and open revolt under the leadership of William, Prince of Orange. By 1572 the Spanish troops had been evicted from many parts of the country and William was proclaimed head of the country or 'Stadholder'. Two years later the last Spanish soldiers left the territory of Holland, never to return. In 1576 the two sides signed a treaty that recognised the status quo with the Dutch in

control of what is now the Netherlands and the Spanish running the territory that is now modern Belgium. Yet that was not the end of the fighting, which flared up sporadically until Dutch independence was formally recognised by the Habsburgs in 1648.

The 17th century was a golden age for the Dutch, whose financiers and merchants led Europe. The year 1602 saw the world's first stock exchange launched in Amsterdam and the foundation of the Dutch East India Company, which built up a wealthy commercial empire in the Far East that survived until the Second World War. Dutch colonists and explorers circled the globe and founded the settlements that later came to be known as Cape Town and New York. Their painters Frans Hals, Rembrandt and Vermeer were the greatest of the time. However, even the worthy burghers of the Netherlands were not immune to flights of fancy and the 16th century saw the frenzy of 'tulipomania' grip the Dutch imagination as thousands of guilders were invested in new varieties of bulbs before the bubble finally burst, leaving many speculators destitute.

The middle years of the 17th century also saw the Dutch in conflict with the British in a series of naval confrontations between the two rising maritime powers of the time. In 1667 the Dutch admiral de Ruyter humiliated the English by burning their fleet as it lay at anchor in the River Medway. However, such conflicts were put aside when the British parliament invited the Dutch head of state, William of Orange, to assume the British crown jointly with his wife Mary in 1688. Under Charles II the British had sided with the French in attacking the Dutch; now they attacked the forces of the Sun King side by side with their new partners.

In the 18th century Britain and the Netherlands went their separate ways. While the British rose to the challenge of industrialisation the Dutch seemed to sink back, locked in the grip of a group of bankers and financiers who were so powerful that for many years they ousted the Orange family from their traditional position as heads of state. The conflict between the bankers and the opposition, known as 'the

THE NETHERLANDS AT A GLANCE

Area 16,042 square miles; land area 13,100 square miles

Population 14,849,100

Capital Amsterdam (seat of government, The Hague)

Government Parliamentary monarchy

Currency Guilder or florin = 100 cents

Languages Dutch, Frisian (minority), but English and German widely spoken

Religion Christian (40% Roman Catholic, 24% Dutch Reformed, 9% other Reformed Churches)

Climate Temperate, maritime; average temperature ranges from –1 to 4°C (30–39°F) in January to 13–22°C (55–72°F) in July

Main primary products Cereals, potatoes, sugar beet, fruit, vegetables, livestock, fish; oil and gas, salt

Major industries Agriculture, food processing, iron and steel, chemicals, textiles, clothing, printing, shipbuilding, tobacco processing, diamond cutting, fertilisers, oil and gas production and refining, fishing

Main exports Food (dairy produce, meat, fruit and vegetables), petroleum products and natural gas, chemicals, machinery, textiles, iron, steel, cut flowers, flower bulbs

Annual income per head (US$) 12,050

Population growth (per thous/ yr) 5

Life expectancy (yrs) Male 73 Female 79

patriots', continued throughout the century and only came to an end when the French Revolutionary Army swept through the Low Countries in 1792.

William V of Orange fled to Britain to avoid capture by the French, who renamed the Netherlands the Batavian Republic. In 1808 Napoleon changed it into the Kingdom of Holland and put his brother Louis on the throne, then changed his mind again in 1810 and incorporated it into the French Empire. With the collapse of Napoleonic power in 1813 the Dutch regained control of their own destiny and William V's remaining son was confirmed as Stadholder.

At the peace congress held in Vienna in 1815 to stabilise Europe after 25 years of war and turmoil, the Stadholder was named King of the United Netherlands, a much larger territory than his ancestors had governed. But 15 years later the southern region, which had very different traditions from the north, rebelled and gained independence and recognition as Belgium.

Steam technology began to have an effect on the Netherlands in 1839 when the railway from Haarlem to Amsterdam was built. The following year steam pumps were used to drain the first large-scale reclamation project of modern times when work started on the 71 square miles of Haarlemmermeer.

The second half of the 19th century was a time of considerable religious turmoil in the Netherlands, and the conflict between Catholics and Calvinists threatened the political stability of the country. Then, about the beginning of the present century, religious mysticism took hold and large numbers of the population became devotees of Theosophy.

The Dutch remained strictly neutral during the First World War and avoided the devastation inflicted on northern France and Belgium. In 1924 they took the first steps toward reclaiming the Zuiderzee, an enormous sea-covered area of land north-east of Amsterdam. One of the first tasks was to build a dam 19 miles long to shut out the sea. It took eight years to complete. Since that time over 625 square miles have been drained, but hundreds of thousands of acres still remain under water.

Dutch neutrality did not save the Netherlands from invasion in 1940. They had no defence against German aerial bombardment and Rotterdam, the country's leading port, was almost completely destroyed. Although Queen Wilhelmina and the government escaped to London, her husband remained behind and was interned by the Germans. The country suffered a second blow the following year when the Japanese overwhelmed their rich colonies in the Far East. In Europe a determined underground resistance movement developed that saved many Allied pilots shot down en route to and from Germany. However, the Allied advance in 1944 bypassed large areas of the Netherlands, leaving the German army of occupation to be rounded up later. Cut off from food supplies during the late winter of 1945, most of the nation came close to starvation and only an extraordinary piece of co-operation between the German command and the British allowed the RAF to drop food for the civilians while fighting was still in progress.

The country's traditional neutrality still affected Dutch politics after the war and NATO had been in existence for five years before the government finally joined the alliance. In the 1980s a vigorous debate raged for years before the government yielded to American pressure to allow nuclear missiles to be stationed in the country.

The Netherlands was not so reticent on the commercial front and, after the loss of the rich resources of Indonesia to the forces of independence, the Dutch first turned to a customs union with Belgium and Luxembourg and then gave wholehearted support to the foundation of the European Community. By the late 1980s they were enthusiastic about further integration. At home the government and city administrations followed enlightened, rational social policies designed to maintain harmony in this small country.

Germany

The historic events which took place in Eastern Europe in autumn 1989 and included the dismantling of the Berlin Wall marked the beginning of a new era for a unified Germany. The country, which has the largest population in the whole of Europe (over 78 million inhabitants), has the highest average standard of living.

Germany has been a rich field for the study of European pre-history. The remains of Stone Age man have been discovered in Neanderthal, Heidelberg and Steinheim. But the first Germans to be included in the historical record were the Teuton and Cimbri tribes who were defeated in 102 BC by the Roman general Marius. Roman expansion was checked when the legions suffered a humiliating reverse at the hands of the German chieftain Hermann in AD 9.

When Roman power waned, the tribes which had remained outside the empire moved south-west to take over the well-cultivated land that was the Roman legacy. These groups fought among themselves until Charlemagne, the leader of the Franks, created an empire that by the end of the 8th century covered most of Germany and France. Only one of his sons remained alive when he died in 814, so the territory passed to Louis intact. But on his death in 843 it was divided among his sons according to Frankish tradition. Rivalry between various local princes helped to fragment what remained. Only under the Hohenstaufen dynasty did the empire experience a resurgence, but after the death of Frederick II in 1250 the empire existed in name only. What remained of the authority of the emperors was continually being contested by the Pope and the local rulers.

Challenges to the authority of the Catholic Church erupted from time to time throughout the Middle Ages, but the most shattering came in 1517 when Martin Luther, a German monk, attacked clerical corruption. The development of the printing press in the previous century had made it easier to spread his views. Soon a movement had been created that was dedicated not so much to the reformation of Catholicism as to the creation of a completely new order – the Protestant Church. Luther's views were adopted by several German princes, probably because he supported their claims to power.

Religious divisions fuelled the political rivalry among the German principalities and fighting was widespread until in 1555 the Treaty of Augsburg codified the right to religious self-determination by each state. Unfortunately the respite was only temporary, and when the Thirty Years' War broke out at the beginning of the next century armies rampaged the length and breadth of Germany. When the country finally sank back exhausted after the Treaty of Westphalia was signed in 1648, Germany was a mosaic of about 300 petty, jealous kingdoms.

One family that had done well out of the carnage were the Hohenzollerns, who ruled Brandenburg. Under Frederick William they expanded their domain until it was known as Brandenburg-Prussia and then made Berlin its capital. Under his grandson, Frederick the Great, Prussia expanded further and came to be regarded as one of Europe's dominant powers. However, after Frederick died in 1786 Prussian power waned and its army was humiliated by Napoleon at the battle of Jena in 1806. This defeat only stiffened Prussian resolve, and within a few years the army was transformed so that under Blücher it combined with the

British under Wellington to defeat the French at Waterloo.

This success greatly strengthened the Prussian hand at the Vienna peace conference and Berlin was able to gain control of more territory, this time on the River Rhine. Prussian power was enhanced further by the customs union they organised with a number of smaller German states in 1834.

The development of democracy in France and Britain during the 19th century had its effect in Germany where petty autocracies could be found everywhere. The growth of nationalism also called these small kingdoms into question. Such sentiments welled up in 1848, a year in which revolt rumbled across Europe, and combined with the discontent of the growing class of industrial workers. In March 1849 a group of political activists gathered in Frankfurt to draft a

constitution for a united Germany. When they offered the crown to Frederick William IV of Prussia he considered their gesture and then dismissed it, sending his troops to attack the gathering. Not until Prince Otto von Bismarck became Chancellor of Prussia in 1862 did a German leader appear who could direct the desire for national unity.

Bismarck's first move was to make war on Denmark to bring the state of Schleswig-Holstein under German control. In 1866 he led Prussia into a trumped-up war with Austria-Hungary which in seven weeks ended forever the ancient empire's claim to German leadership. In 1867 Bismarck created a North German Confederation that lined up many of the small states behind Berlin's leadership. Finally, in 1870 the 'Iron Chancellor' provoked Napoleon III into declaring war. The Prussian army humiliated the French and in March 1871 the Prussian king was crowned Emperor of a united Germany in the Hall of Mirrors in Versailles.

The open market of a united Germany proved to be an enormous stimulus to the country's industrial machine; production increased 43 per cent in the decade to 1880 and another 64 per cent during the next ten years. Lacking the inertia of established industrial plant that Britain possessed, Germany could invest immediately in the new technologies such as steel, electrical plant and automobiles that were emerging at the end of the 19th century. Meanwhile, in the 1880s Bismarck was out-flanking the demands of the growing industrial work-force and their socialist representatives by giving them health and accident insurance, as well as old-age pensions. However, the old fox was too much for the impetuous new Emperor (Kaiser) Wilhelm II, who in 1890 dismissed him, and from that point kept the control of events largely in his own hands.

Where Bismarck had been careful not to antagonise the other major European powers once German unity was established, Wilhelm's strutting pomposity soon annoyed rival powers. His enthusiasm for an enlarged naval building programme so alarmed the British that both nations were soon locked in an arms race. The threat of his army drove France and Russia into an alliance less than 40 years after they had been at each other's throats in the Crimea. By the early 20th century the European powers were involved in political alliances and rivalries that brought them close to war almost annually. In retrospect it is surprising that the First World War did not occur sooner.

Germany was dragged into the fray through the Austro-Hungarian Empire's confrontation with Serbia, a small Slav nation in the Balkans that sheltered under Russia's protective wing. The mobilisation of each nation after the Austrian Archduke and his wife were assassinated by a Serbian nationalist, provoked similar moves by its neighbours. The German government believed that they were faced with a rerun of 1870 and that a swift strike through Belgium would knock out France while Britain remained neutral.

Berlin's assumptions might well have been proved right had Britain stood aside but its regular army's key role in the first battle of the Marne denied the Germans access to Paris when they were almost in artillery range. The war in the west became bogged down in the stalemate of trench warfare for four years. German successes on the eastern front against Russia, where the fighting was more mobile, were much greater, but Berlin did not have the resources to win in the east and hold the Anglo-French threat in the west at the same time.

Although it only worked very slowly, the British naval blockade slowly brought Germany to its knees and when German submarine strikes provoked the Americans into declaring war, the end was in sight. After one last desperate push by the Germans in March 1918 their army collapsed, and an armistice was agreed by November of that year.

The German public were bewildered. With two million of their men dead on the battlefield and nothing to show for

years of hardship and privation, they were looking for scapegoats. The first to go was the Kaiser, who ended his days in exile in the Netherlands.

A democratically elected government had to be established to conduct the peace negotiations, a task not calculated to endear it to its people. France in particular would be satisfied with nothing less than vengeance and sought to impose the toughest terms it could. Germany was forced to cede territory and pay enormous sums in compensation. When the weakened German economy collapsed under the strain in 1923, Paris ordered its troops to occupy the Ruhr to enforce French demands. This only hastened the further disintegration of the German economy and its currency became totally worthless. Only after Gustav Stresemann was appointed Chancellor in that year was a government established that brought stability to Germany and a measure of prosperity. In the end the French had no alternative but to let their demands for massive compensation drop quietly from public notice.

In 1929 the economic bubble burst when the Wall Street Crash destroyed business confidence inside the United States and millions were thrown out of work. This had a catastrophic effect on the German economy and nearly six million people were soon unemployed. In its bewilderment the German public turned to the demagogue who shouted loudest, and Adolf Hitler's National Socialist Party – the Nazis – soon became the largest party in parliament. However, by 1932 the German people were showing signs of tiring of Hitler's rhetoric and his party lost seats in the election of that year. To secure his position he engineered a crisis and then cajoled the country's President into appointing him Chancellor.

Now that he had his hands on the levers of power, Hitler began intimidating and murdering his enemies both inside and outside his party. Leaders of German industry and the army thought that they could control Hitler, disposing of him when he became tiresome. However, public works measures put in hand by the previous government began to have an effect and Hitler took the credit for their success, increasing his popularity. His next step was to leave the League of Nations, the forerunner of the United Nations set up after the First World War, and promote a rearmament programme. This gave him the confidence to take a calculated risk in 1936 and send troops into the neutral Rhineland. When he encountered no opposition from foreign governments he grew bolder. In 1938 he annexed Austria and then claimed a part of Czechoslovakia where a large section of the population spoke German. Very poor British military intelligence encouraged Whitehall to appease Hitler on the grounds that the Czechs would be unable to resist. German military intelligence knew better, but London and Paris gave way and Hitler anticipated no trouble over his invasion of Poland in 1939. Britain's unexpected decision to stand firm precipitated the Second World War.

After its easy conquest of Poland, the German High Command waited until the spring of 1940 before unleashing its attack to the west. In a matter of weeks all opposition in western Europe was swept aside and Britain was isolated. After an unsuccessful attempt to gain control of British air space and so prepare the way for an invasion, Hitler turned his attention to his final objective – the conquest of the Soviet Union.

In the summer of 1941 German troops rolled eastward but, like the French in 1812, they found the distances too great for a quick victory to be possible. Soviet troops just retreated and then counter-attacked in the depths of winter. The summer of 1942 saw further German advances but the Red Army refused to concede and in massive tank battles that ranged over hundreds of miles won crucial victories the following year. The loss of the 6th Army at Stalingrad was the last straw for the Germans, and after the D-Day

GERMANY AT A GLANCE

Area 137,845 square miles

Population 78,656,100

Capital Berlin

Government Federal republic

Currency Deutschmark = 100 Pfennig

Languages German

Religion Christian (37% Protestant, 49% Roman Catholic), Muslim minority

Climate Temperate; average temperatures in Berlin range from −1 to 20°C (30–68°F)

Main primary products Cereals, potatoes, sugar beet, fruit and vegetables, livestock, milk and milk products, wine, timber, fish; coal, lignite, oil and natural gas, iron ore, potash, zinc, lead, salt

Major industries Iron, steel and non-ferrous metals, mining, petroleum products, chemicals, motor vehicles, aircraft, machine tools, electrical and electronic equipment, computers, textiles, ceramics, glass, cement, agriculture, food processing, forestry, fishing

Main exports Machinery, motor vehicles, chemicals, iron and steel, food, small metal manufactures, textile yarns and fabrics, instruments

Population growth (per thous/ yr) Declining

Life expectancy (yrs) Male 72 Female 79

landings, their final defeat was only a matter of time as they tried to defend themselves on two fronts.

Germany's collapse in 1945 was total. After the surviving Nazi leaders had been tried at Nuremburg, France, Britain, America and the Soviet Union each administered its own zone of occupation. The Americans were keen to learn from the mistakes of the 1920s and gave large amounts of aid under the Marshall Plan so that Germany could rebuild its cities and industries. When the western allies sponsored a plan for currency reform in 1948, the Soviet Union imposed a blockade on Berlin that was only overcome by a massive airlift of supplies. This combined effort encouraged the western allies to trust the Germans in their zones and after the lifting of the blockade in May 1949 progress was soon made in the setting up of the Federal Republic. The Soviet Union responded by turning their zone into the German Democratic Republic.

The first elections in the west in August 1949 gave the Christian Democrats under Konrad Adenauer a small majority. They stayed in power until 1966, presiding over the signing of the Treaty of Rome and other moves towards greater European co-operation. By the start of the 1960s West Germany was becoming a prosperous country. Meanwhile, the East was nationalising its industry and distributing land to peasant farms, who were then organised into collective farms. A mass revolt against this system in June 1953 was brutally repressed. However, the border between East and West was still open and many skilled workers and professional people migrated. To stem this brain drain, the East fortified the border and built the Berlin Wall.

Between 1966 and 1969 West Germany was governed by a coalition until fresh elections made the socialist Willy Brandt chancellor. He initiated a less suspicious attitude towards eastern Europe which culminated in a treaty with East Germany that ratified their common border and established diplomatic relations between the two countries. Both were then admitted to the United Nations.

The arrest of one of Brandt's aides as a spy in 1974 brought the Chancellor's resignation, but his party stayed in power until 1982. The country's growing respectability in the international community and the continuing increase in its prosperity tipped the balance of power in its favour within the European Community after de Gaulle resigned as French President.

The reunification of Germany officially took place on October 3, 1990, four decades after the country was divided by the World War Allies. The events leading up to this historic date were observed by the world with hope and anticipation for what was to come. When Hungary opened its borders with Austria the influx of refugees from east to west was massive. In the first quarter of 1989, 240,000 East Germans emigrated to the West.

The Communist leadership gradually lost political power and economic control as popular unrest and pressure for reform grew. On October 18, Erich Honecker was replaced after 16 years as Communist leader by Egon Krenz. The border between East and West Germany was finally opened on November 9, 1989 in an effort to prevent the gradual depopulation of East Germany.

Early in 1990, the Federal Republic and the German Democratic Republic, along with the Allies, agreed that reunification talks should begin. East German elections were held on March 18, 1990 and resulted in a resounding vote for reunification. On October 3, East and West Germany were officially united. The results of the first united elections in December gave victory to the Christian Democratic Union and Helmut Kohl, who became the first Chancellor of the reunited Germany.

The economic and political difficulties facing Germany were complex and manifold. The enormous gap in levels of economic development between the two former German states led many to doubt the ability of the country to assimilate the East without major setbacks.

Many argued that monetary union, which was introduced in July 1990, would cause deflation in the East and inflation in the West. The matter was resolved when a one-to-one conversion rate between Eastern and Western marks was agreed on and the currency of West Germany, the Deutschmark, was introduced as the common currency.

Reunification in political terms means greater responsibilities for Germany on the international front. These responsibilities include commitment to European integration, East–West co-operation and Third World development. A unified Germany has introduced a new perspective to East–West relations and the opportunity to enhance contacts with Eastern Europe.

Switzerland

Switzerland is a country that fought to gain its independence before its neighbours and has maintained its integrity down the centuries, despite the turbulence of wars and alliances in the surrounding lands.

Like most of western Europe it endured the arrival and departure of the Celts, the Romans, the nomadic tribes from the east and the empire of Charlemagne. However, under the Franks the local communities of the region, known as cantons, were allowed considerable independence. This made the intrusion of the Habsburgs in the 12th and 13th centuries more unacceptable because their style of government was dictatorial and harsh. As a result three of the cantons – Schwyz, Unterwalden and Uri – signed a compact in 1291, known as the Perpetual Edict, to rid themselves of the Habsburgs. Within 25 years they had succeeded and they were joined in the struggle by Lucerne, Zurich and Berne. However, it was not until 1499 that the combined efforts of the cantons forced the Habsburgs to sign the Treaty of Basel in which the imperial family accepted Swiss self-government.

Within a generation this hard-won independence was placed at risk by the religious controversies of the Reformation. Some cantons remained Catholic while in others the population became Protestants. The presence of Calvin and Zwingli, two of the most vigorous prophets of the new faith, merely antagonised those cantons that retained their allegiance to Rome.

By 1648, in the Treaty of Westphalia which ended the Thirty Years' War, the rest of Europe acknowledged the right of the Swiss to their independence. However, the country was still no more than a loose confederation of bickering cantons without any effective central government.

During the French Revolution the Swiss tried to aid Louis XVI, so it is not surprising that when the revolutionary armies went on the offensive they invaded Switzerland and installed a puppet regime. Only with the final defeat of

Napoleon and the Treaty of Vienna in 1815 did the Swiss regain their independence. Their neutral status was now guaranteed by all the major European powers.

After their return to self-government some Swiss wished to overhaul their constitution and establish an effective central administration. The split between reformers and conservatives became aligned along religious lines with Protestants advocating change and the Catholics resisting it. Passions rose until they boiled over into a brief civil war in 1847, in which the Catholic alliance, known as the Sonderbund, was defeated and the enthusiasts for more effective central government carried the day. In the new constitution the federal government was elected directly on the basis of one man, one vote. Women were not enfranchised until 1971. The cantons retained many of their powers, while serious and divisive national issues were to be put to the electorate, to be settled by referenda.

The country's internal stability and its avoidance of armed conflict with other nations helped to ensure that during the 19th century it became one of the world's most prosperous nations, a status it still enjoys. In the 1870s it invested in the new technology that allowed it to take over from Clerkenwell in London as the world's watch-making centre. Such stability also attracted the growing number of international institutions that have sprouted since the middle of the 19th century, starting with the Red Cross which was founded by a Swiss, Jean Henri Dunant, in 1864. This was followed by the arrival of the headquarters of the League of Nations after the First World War. Even though the country refused to join the United Nations on the grounds that its neutrality would be compromised, Switzerland has still managed since 1945 to attract the offices of many of the subsidiary organisations of the world body. Its rules on confidentiality have also attracted many banks and although the country is not a host to the world's major trading markets, its banking services continue to attract large amounts of capital to this small but industrious nation.

SWITZERLAND AT A GLANCE

Area 15,943 square miles

Population 6,723,500

Capital Berne

Government Federal republic

Currency Swiss franc, or franken = 100 centimes or rappen

Languages German, French, Italian, Romansch

Religion Christian (48% Roman Catholic, 44% Protestant)

Climate Warm summers, cold winters; average temperature in Zurich ranges from –3 to 2°C (27–36°F) in January to 13–24°C (55–75°F) in July

Main primary products Wheat, barley, potatoes, grapes, apples, livestock, timber; salt, building stone

Major industries Tourism, machinery, chemicals, pharmaceuticals, banking and insurance, clock- and watch-making, instruments, textiles and yarns, forestry, paper and wood pulp, cement, iron and steel

Main exports Machinery, chemicals, pharmaceuticals, precious metals and jewellery, clocks and watches, instruments, textiles, food

Annual income per head (US$) 19,250

Population growth (per thous/yr) 2.8

Life expectancy (yrs) Male 73 Female 80

Austria

Austria today is best known to many tourists as a holiday location, with skiing as the attraction in the winter and the Salzburg music festival in the summer. But this small, mountainous country strewn with pretty villages was once the home of one of the great ruling dynasties of history.

People first settled in Austria during the Stone Age and by 500 BC the area was the centre of a thriving civilisation. When the Romans invaded in 15 BC it took them 25 years to

bring under control the region they called Noricum. As in so many parts of Europe, Rome's collapse was followed by the arrival of nomadic tribes from the east. Only when Charlemagne took over the region did stability return to this mountainous country.

In 976 much of what is now modern Austria passed into the hands of the Babenberg family. The last of the Babenbergs was killed in a battle with the Magyars in 1246 and the region became the scene of dynastic rivalry for almost 40 years. Only when the Habsburgs took control of part of the region did a degree of stability return.

Originally the Habsburgs were an aristrocratic family with their roots in Alsace and Switzerland, who owned a little land in Austria. However, in 1282 a German member of the family, Rudolf of Habsburg, defeated the Bohemians, taking from them the provinces of Austria and Styria which he gave to his sons. This branch of the family extended its holdings and its income through marriage alliances with the royal families of Europe. As a consequence, by the end of the 15th century the Habsburgs held property scattered throughout Europe and were frequently elected to hold the honorary title of Holy Roman Emperor which had first been given to Charlemagne.

In the Middle East the Ottoman Empire was growing so fast that its thrust northwards was starting to threaten central Europe. In 1529 the Turks attacked Vienna and, although the siege was lifted, the invaders retained control of parts of what is now Hungary until the end of the 17th century. In 1683 the Turks and the Magyars combined to attack the Habsburgs, besieging Vienna again. This siege was only broken by the arrival of a relief column from Germany and Poland, by which time the Turkish engineers had made substantial progress in mining under the city walls.

While the Habsburgs had been preoccupied with their southern neighbours, Prussian power had been growing to their north. In 1740 the Emperor Charles VI died, leaving no male heir. However, he wanted his daughter Maria Theresa to succeed him even though women were barred from the imperial throne. To circumvent this restriction he had persuaded all the European powers to sign a waiver acknowledging her right to succeed. But that did not stop Frederick the Great trying to extend Prussian power by invading the empire and taking Silesia. Then France intervened to support Charles Albert of Bavaria's claim to the throne. The Empress survived this pressure, which continued for eight years, only through a stubborn refusal to concede and the help of an alliance with Holland and Britain, and reigned until her death in 1780.

Maria Theresa's son Joseph II lived for only ten years after succeeding to the throne. Joseph was a keen patron of the arts, favouring the opera and the theatre. His era and the years that followed saw Vienna at the height of its prestige as the music capital of Europe. This was the time of Haydn and Mozart, who were followed by Beethoven and Schubert; each spent many years in the Austrian capital.

War broke out between France and Austria in April 1792 and rumbled on for many years. Although the Austrians and their Prussian allies scored early successes, they were soon thrown back. As the years passed the Habsburgs lost a lot of territory and much prestige, particularly while Napoleon ruled France. They were expelled from northern Italy and the Rhineland. At Austerlitz, in 1805, they were the victims of one of Napoleon's most crushing victories. After another major defeat at Wagram in 1809 the empire was completely humiliated and only the skill of Prince Metternich, the German whom the Emperor appointed as his foreign minister, raised Austria's prestige in the years that followed. It was Metternich who organised the Congress of Vienna in 1815, which settled the outstanding issues between the major European powers.

In March 1848 revolution erupted onto the streets of Vienna. The Emperor, Ferdinand I, had been forced to concede a liberal constitution by the revolutionaries. When he replaced Metternich with a new chief minister, the latter ordered the army to attack and Ferdinand abdicated. He was replaced by his nephew Franz Joseph, whose 68-year reign witnessed the final collapse of Austrian power.

The year 1866 was the next milestone on the empire's road to dissolution. Austria's financial situation was very weak and lack of investment undermined the army. The empire was provoked into war by Bismarck and the Prussians. The result was a crushing defeat at the hands of the Prussian army at Sadowa in July 1866.

With the empire on the ropes, the Hungarians demanded autonomy and acquired their own government based in Budapest. As the century drew to a close Slav nationalism also found its voice, encouraged by the Russians. During the first decade of the 20th century these undercurrents surfaced in a great deal of unrest that led directly to the murder of Archduke Franz Ferdinand, the heir to the imperial crown. The assassination brought to the surface all the tensions and rivalries that led to the First World War. Little had changed in 50 years and the imperial forces were as weak as ever. Austrian society was in little better shape and the imperial government finally collapsed as the war came to an end.

The inter-war years were an unhappy time for Austria. Civil war threatened in the 1920s and broke out in 1934. The leader of the ruling Catholic party, Engelbert Dollfuss, quickly crushed the socialists and announced a dictatorship. But within months he was murdered by one of Hitler's Austrian supporters. In 1938 Germany invaded Austria, announcing that they had created a 'Greater Germany'.

After the Second World War the Allies occupied the country and divided it into four zones, as in Germany. Only in 1955 was it allowed to resume its independence and then only on the condition that it remained neutral, a situation that remains to this day.

AUSTRIA AT A GLANCE

Area 32,375 square miles

Population 7,624,000

Capital Vienna

Government Parliamentary republic

Currency Schilling = 100 groschen

Languages German (99%), plus 1% Magyar and Slovene

Religion Christian (88% Roman Catholic)

Climate Temperate continental; average temperature in Vienna ranges from –4 to 1°C (25–34°F) in January to 15–25°C (59–77°F) in July

Main primary products Cattle, sheep, wheat, maize, potatoes, hay and fodder, barley, sugar beet, grapes, temperate fruits, timber; oil and natural gas, lignite, iron ore, magnesite, graphite

Major industries Agriculture, iron and steel, machinery, forestry and wood products, chemicals, textiles, oil and gas production and refining, wine, beer, food processing

Main exports Iron and steel, machinery, timber and wood products, chemicals, textiles, meat and dairy produce

Annual income per head (US$) 8,750

Population growth (per thous/yr) 1.1

Life expectancy (yrs) Male 71 Female 78

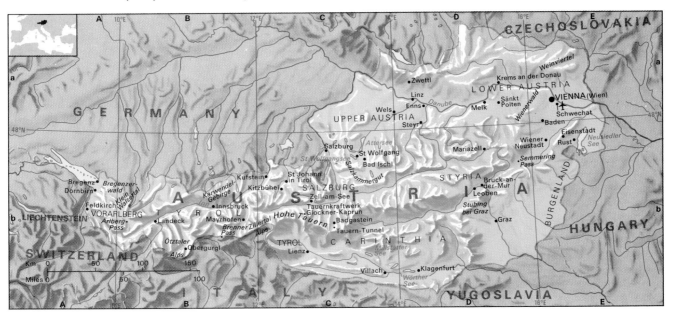

Picture credits